UNHEARD
SCREAMS

A True Childhood Horror Story
of a CODA Survivor and How She Overcame
Her Father's Sexual Abuse

MORGAN CRITZER

Unheard Screams: A True Childhood Horror Story of a CODA Survivor and How She Overcame Her Father's Sexual Abuse

Trilogy Christian Publishers
A Wholly Owned Subsidary of Trinity Broadcasting Network
2442 Michelle Drive, Tustin, CA 92780

10 9 8 7 6 5 4 3 2 1
Library of Congress Cataloging-in-Publication Data is available.

ISBN 979-8-89041-465-6
ISBN 979-8-89041-466-3 (ebook)

DEDICATION

I dedicate this book to my deaf brother, Ted, and late sister, Dottie (1970–2022). My fraternal twin siblings and I had different journeys that led to further dysfunction and destruction. The state-run child protective services separated us into two different foster homes. Ted had undergone unthinkable abuse from his first foster home. Furthermore, the state transferred my brother and sister to live with our father, leading to further abuse. Dottie became my father's target throughout her childhood and teen years, leading her to sexual immorality, heavy drug addictions, and alcoholism, which eventually destroyed her and took her life. It was upon learning about my sister's recent death that my brother and I were finally restored. Today, I am very thankful that God preserved him. He is married to a wonderful deaf woman, Arica.

To my beloved children, Brooke, Levi, and Jeremiah. By the grace of God, it has always been my wholehearted pursuit to give you the best life, help push you forward using your God-given gifts and talents and become all that God has created you to be. All this I did for you so that you would never know what I had known.

— Love, Mom

ACKNOWLEDGMENTS

To my seminary alumna friend, Jessica Padilla, for encouraging me to write this book.

A huge thank you to my counselor and friend, Michelle Alexander, who opened my eyes for the first time to see my true identity and worth in Christ Jesus. She was the first stepping stone in helping reroute my path of spiritual abuse and dysfunctional marriage, pulling me out of legalism and pointing me in the right direction. I now walk a Spirit-filled life full of God's favor and grace. I could not have done this without her.

To my long-time college best friend, Christine Dixon, who never gave up on me; even when it seemed like I had fallen off the face of the earth, she scoured every place, turned over every stone to search for me, and eventually found me. I thank her and her husband, Bill, for their support in reviewing my book before publication. I am also thankful to Christine's mom, Pam, for cheering me on and taking the place of a surrogate mother.

I sincerely want to thank my late foster mother, Ele Baxter (February 8, 2022), for her sacrifices of love. I dedicate the hymn song "In the Garden" to her. It was a song that we were supposed to sing together in 1987 at the Augusta Methodist Church.

Ele gave me wonderful opportunities I never had during my youth. She amazingly condensed the best life I could ever imagine, all in over two years. May God richly reward her in heaven for ministering to me and to every girl she took in under her care.

The two verses that best fit Ele's description are found in Mark 9:41, "For whoever gives you a cup of water to drink in My name, because you belong to Christ, assuredly, I say to you, he will by no means lose his reward."

> Then the King will say to those on His right hand, "Come, you blessed of My Father, inherit the kingdom prepared for you from the foundation of the world: for I was hungry and you gave Me food; I was thirsty and you gave Me drink; I was a stranger and you took Me in; I *was* naked and you clothed Me; I was sick and you visited Me; I was in prison and you came to Me."
> Then the righteous will answer Him, saying, "Lord, when did we see You hungry and feed *You*, or thirsty and give *You* drink? When did we see You a stranger and take *You* in, or naked and clothe *You?* Or when did we see You sick, or in prison, and come to You?" And the King will answer and say to them, "Assuredly, I say to you, inasmuch as you did *it* to one of the least of these My brethren, you did *it* to Me."
>
> Matthew 25:34–40

To my former high school classmate, Jackie Kelly, who chose my first name, *Morgan*—the name change turned over a new leaf and transformed my life—a sincere "Thank you" for being a true friend.

A huge shout-out to my high school creative writing teacher, Mrs. Nancy Emmerich. She was the first teacher who cared and inspired me to express my ideas using words on paper. Her enthusiasm for writing was contagious. In an instant, I caught the bug.

Thank you to my dear, compassionate friend, Richard Samuel from Asbury Seminary, who stepped in as my elder brother. He comforted me and read the Scriptures whenever I needed consolation. I never will forget so many times that he told me in his thick Indian accent, "You're never alone, Morgie."

To this day, Richard and his wife are missionaries in their homeland in India with the support of a Christian ministry, Fishhook International. They rescue disposed babies, orphaned children, and destitute women by providing food, shelter, jobs, and educational training programs. They also mentor and train leaders to launch sustainable community development initiatives. Learn more at www.fishhook.org.

I am forever indebted to Luke and Lois Byers, who stood in the gap for me, for truth's sake. Thank you!

A huge thanks to my friends and extended family members: Faith Trollinger, Naomi Coronado, Amy Upton, LaRae Parsons, Jeffrey Scott, Kim and Minesh Baxi, Dan Carr, Darcy Bridgeman, Patty Tomlinson, and Edith & Bryce Mogriff, for your love, friendship, prayers, and support.

A big thank you to my counselor, Jackie, from Lakewood Church, who took the time to listen and gave me wise counsel and resources to help my spiritual growth. Each time I heard her pray over me, it gave me a spiritual boost and encouragement to move forward.

Pheobe and Zara, my Goldendoodles, have been my constant, loyal companions and emotional support while I wrote this book. I genuinely do not know what I would have done without them.

Finally, I thank Jesus Christ for the finished work on the cross so I could be set free. Through Him, I have been given everything I need to overcome and to be all He has created me to be. This same Jesus who willingly took all my dysfunctions, traumas, sexual abuse, emotional abuse, and spiritual abuse has crucified them upon His body as a legal transactional exchange so I could be healed, restored, and live an abundant life. Today, I am the righteousness of God in Christ Jesus.

I thank God in heaven for being my "Abba" Father when I never had a loving father figure. Throughout my life, His right hand has always held onto mine and has never let go.

INTRODUCTION

There are many stories in the New Testament about Jesus performing miracles and healing people. Those who were healed went back to their families and to the cities where they came from to tell everyone everything about what Jesus had done for them.

In John Chapter 4, there is one story about a woman at the well. She had five husbands and was living with a man. Jesus made it a priority to go see her. In verse 4, it says, "But He needed to go through Samaria." The woman often went to the well at noontime when no one was around. Most people drew water from the well during the early cool mornings. Therefore, the woman preferred to be unseen because she didn't feel loved or belonged. Each day, she went alone, drawing water with her water pot. She had preferred to suffer the noonday heat than to suffer criticism and rejection from people.

During one of those hot noon days, Jesus sat by the well. The woman approached Him, realizing that He was not from the area. With deep compassion and love, Jesus foretold precisely about the woman's past regarding her five ex-husbands and the man whom she was presently living with. He did not condemn her, but instead, He offered her eternal springs of living water. She said, "Give me this water, that I may not thirst, nor come here to draw."

Moreover, despite her messy past, Jesus lovingly shared with her that He was the Messiah. The once condemned and shamed woman who hid from everyone could not contain herself anymore. She dropped her waterpot and went back to the city to proclaim about Jesus. Many people who heard her share about what transpired at the well believed and followed Christ, the Savior of the world. (See John 4:1–42.)

Similarly, as the woman at the well shared her story in her city, I am sharing my testimony to the world of the great things that Jesus has done in my life. Regardless of who you are, if you have lost all hope and faith, God has never abandoned you.

This is a true story of my childhood and throughout my young adult years. Despite everything I have gone through, I still stand as a living, breathing trophy of grace today. I want to give you, the reader, a glimpse of what goes on behind closed doors in a domestic, sexually abusive home and also in spiritually abusive churches because things are not always what they seem. I have experienced every form of abuse imaginable, along with a plethora of family and other relationship dysfunctions. As a believer, I struggled for a very long time to believe that I was part of the body of Christ because I didn't feel welcomed or like I belonged in the circle of believers and in the churches I attended. I shared this struggle with my counselor. She broadened my perspective and said that I was part of the body of Christ worldwide. She was right. The body of Christ does not consist of two hundred people in a church. It's bigger than that. The roadblock in my mind was removed, and this new perspective allowed me to see God in a bigger way than I ever imagined. I had to walk in faith and believe that I was part of and still have a part in God's extended family of faith-filled believers around the globe. God's thoughts about me in the Scriptures were different than what people thought about me.

I had to take that leap of faith and believe that I am a member of the body of Christ. (See 1 Corinthians 12:12–27.)

The abuse I went through was so traumatizing that even through my adult years, that little girl inside me was still hurting. Deep down, those traumas were being rehearsed repeatedly in my mind. It felt like I was unable to cope with life because that was all I knew growing up. I found ways to hide that little girl through overeating and sexual immorality to pacify my pain. That little girl inside me was an overachiever and did everything perfectly to please people, but it wasn't good enough.

I wholeheartedly tried to leave the past behind me and walk in faith as a born-again believer in Christ Jesus. As a Christian, I had entrusted my whole life to the hands of those who considered themselves spiritual authorities, and I even followed their rules and traditions to the best of my ability.

I attended denominational churches that tried to push their doctrines down my throat. I also went to other churches that based their teachings on Bill Gothard. It was so strict that these religious groups followed every rule from Gothard's "Basic Life Principles." I went to the Bill Gothard seminars, and it was so convincing that it caused me to steer off the path of the Word of God. The rules according to Gothard had no biblical foundation. It was nothing but principles or manmade opinions that were distractions. It consumed me and took away my relationship with Jesus. Instead of learning the Word of God, I was learning about rules. It was so daunting that I had to focus on making sure that the length of my skirt was acceptable. Whenever I wore shorts, it was demanded to be worn precisely below the knee. There were also rules about music. Every Christian and gospel singer who had drums in their group was considered evil. The list went on and on. The church leaders took Bible verses out of context and used them as weapons to create fear and control. In my experience, this is considered spiritual abuse. I lived in a state of anxiety, fear, and deeper shame. I started to hate myself and my body because the religious leaders laser-focused on women as the fault and problem of causing all men to fall into immorality. After many years, I realized too late, and everything in my life fell apart and was destroyed.

There was not one person that I could talk to about my past and present circumstances to help lead me forward to victory in Christ. As a female, I was brainwashed to believe that I had no rights, nor could I share my feelings. I trusted the religious leaders because they gave the impression that they knew everything. I had believed that submitting myself without questioning them and following their rules was the only ticket and way to heaven.

When I chose to follow Jesus, I truly believed that I would have a better life, but it turned out to be my worst nightmare. The churches I attended were supposed to be like lighthouses that shine brightly to rescue and help the fatherless, the lost, and the weary, but they turned me away. They became unsafe places. I was tormented by their oppressive rules and legalism. They shackled me into a dark prison of hopelessness. The rigidness and criticism of the religious leaders created an impression in my life that God was out to get me and that He was mad at me all the time.

There was so much strife and division in the churches of God. Families and friendships were destroyed. As much as I tried to fit into their perfect mold, I was neglected and despised. Shame and fear were the foundation of these churches. The religious leaders kept very private lives but would shame those who dared to expose or confront them. They used scare tactics to force me to submit against my will. I felt I had no choice because they often brought in more people to purposefully band together as a form of intimidation to break me. They did this to other believers, too. This method encouraged them because they wanted power and control. Even though I was already a broken person from my past, Satan worked overtime through them to break my spirit. It worked, and during those many years, my spiritual life was nothing but a shattered mess and a pile of ashes. I became dehumanized. The religious leaders believed that they were mandated by God to break people's spirits by using any method possible. They also believed in breaking the will and spirit of every child, even as young as nine months old. A blanket training technique was used for babies to break their will and spirit, as suggested through Gothard's teachings. It broke my heart to see my oldest son, who was only nine months old at the time, go through that process. He cried uncontrollably, gasping for air as if his heart was broken. As a mother, I was not allowed to have any say, nor did I have any rights. Spanking babies by using the blanket training technique is not sound and not biblically based; it is abuse. Being exposed to these false teachings created confusion in my life.

Satan was on a mission to destroy me because, deep down, I loved Jesus. I knew something was not right, but I was stuck and drowning in the swamp. I believed that Jesus was the way, the truth, and the life, but these religious leaders led me to hopelessness, despair, and defeat. In turn, I became angry, rageful, bitter, and frustrated. I found myself alone and wished that I had never existed, but deep down inside, there was a flicker of light left inside of me. I was still anchored to Jesus Christ. For those who have jumped ship from these kinds of churches, I'm sure you can relate to what I'm talking about.

Trauma is the most challenging thing to live with. Everything was so messy. Nothing made any sense. Sexual, emotional, and even spiritual abusers formed my identity; therefore, I did not know who I was. Once, one of my spiritual abusers laughed at me and pointed out that I did not know who I was. He was right because he did not know how to point me and show me who I was in Christ. He was a blind leader leading blind people.

My journey has had many pitfalls, but Jesus was always there. Even though I felt alone, He never abandoned me. Throughout my life, He sent specific people to help encourage and push me forward. However, some people used me and God to their advantage. When I say they used God, I mean to say that they used the words from the Scriptures out of context for their gain and control. They cloaked themselves with sheepskin and forged God's Word into their own formulated manufactured opinions to appear righteous, yet underneath the counterfeit costume, they were wolves all along. These religious people made it hard for me to move forward. They loaded me with rules I had to follow in order to make it to heaven. As a Christian, even though I was forgiven and my identity in Christ is declared in the Scriptures, religious people viewed me as a messed-up victim and compared me to my father and mother, even though I walked away from that past life. Religious people chained me to my past and never declared who

I was in Christ. Please, do not blame God for all your misfortunes. Blame Satan. He is your enemy and will appear as an angel of light working through people. He seeks to steal, to kill, and to destroy your life. Jesus came to save you and give you an abundant life.

If you have been abused and face religious people who lump your entire past and claim it as their view of you, you must leave those people and find another church. The religious leaders hated Jesus, too.

It is so easy to have compassion and help people with physical limitations. But, for those who have been traumatically abused, it's different.

Emotional wounds cut deeper than physical wounds. People cannot see emotional pain more than they can physical pain. It is easier to offer help to someone hobbling on crutches than to someone limping emotionally wearing an unseen, invisible backpack filled with past abuse.

I thank God that He used my biological family and religious people to push me down to the bottom of the pit because it only caused me to spring back up and move forward to my destiny. I did not know it then, but, looking back, I am amazed at His divine intervention and miracles in my life.

All that changed when Jesus stepped in and rescued me on the day I left jail in 2015. My counselor, Michelle Alexander, was an instrument of God who helped me to see my identity in Christ. This rocked my world. I was consistently told by a religious person that I was a rebellious and unsubmitted woman, and he said that God mandated him to put his thumb on me until I submitted. That was his whole focus and nothing else. I was already a broken person. Submitting myself to this form of spiritual abuse was a vice that Satan wanted to use to destroy me.

When I was trying to seek Jesus, I had many oppositions. It felt like they did not want me to change. Instead, they tried to keep me stuck in my past. Even when I continued to believe them and serve in the church, I felt empty. Religious people impacted my life spiritually negatively, and I was often told that I was going to hell. I was trapped. They were harsh; therefore, my perception of God was a mean God. They defined the framework of how faithful Christians should behave based on legalism and their personal opinions but based everything according to the teachings of Bill Gothard's "Basic Life Principles." They did not base Christianity on the true Word of God. I have watched many people jump ship from churches I attended and even witnessed many marriages and families destroyed. My faith was often shaken because of the false teachings and misguidance of those with no discernment in the body of Christ.

Even though I was saved as a young teenager and later went to seminary, I did not know who I was in Christ. I was taught biblical history and other doctrines, yet there was no teaching on our identity in Christ, nor did we learn about the grace of Jesus Christ. The word "grace" was defined by these teachers and leaders as a negative word. For many years, I became more and more confused with the gospel in the New Testament. It was a blur because the word "grace" was detached from it, and legalism, or the "law," replaced it. God was painted out to be a distant Old Testament figure who was a fierce and angry God. The religious leaders never taught about who we were in Christ. Jesus finished the work on the cross and blessed us with favor and grace, but as believers, we had to follow the rules and follow manufactured opinions.

I attended various denominations and non-denominational churches but was never shepherded correctly. It never felt like I was living in green pastures. Something was missing in the churches that I attended. I desired to do what was right and wholeheartedly loved Jesus, but most Christians in my past did not display the love of Christ for me to follow their example. It caused confusion and frustration in my walk with the Lord. It was like the blind leading the blind and falling into a pit. Christian carnage was strewn everywhere, and the church terrain was nothing but an empty, desolate wasteland. I stumbled and fell so many times. It was a slow, bumpy process, but by God's grace, He lifted me from the pit. As a young believer trying to find my way, I felt that there were many strongholds around these denominational and non-denominational churches. These walls must come down. Otherwise, these churches will become an unkept, stinky sheep pen of underfed and neglected sheep. See Ezekiel Chapter 34.

From my experience and having lived under the broken state-run foster care system, I have witnessed many abused children coming in and out of my first former foster home. If it weren't for Jesus, I would have ended up a statistic. Many sources can tell you that these foster children end up with drug addictions, committing suicide, and even repeating the same cycle of abuse in their future relationships. I was blessed to live with a Christian foster mother. Yet, there are children who end up being shuffled around through the state-run foster care system. Once they are weaned out from foster care, many of them end up homeless and don't have the life skills to begin a new life.

I can also testify that while Satan is busy working overtime to destroy the body of Christ from the inside out, its light becomes more diminished. As a former abuse survivor, I have observed many Christians detouring away from their purposes in life. They spend their time fighting and bickering amongst themselves over petty things. It took me over forty-five years to find my way out of the darkness, even while I was attending different churches. The church has lost its saltiness. In this most critical time in church history, broken and lost young people are looking for answers. As the world gets darker and darker, may the church, by God's grace, shine brighter and brighter by being the hands and feet of Jesus to heal and restore them back to wholeness.

> Then Jesus went about all the cities and villages, teaching in their synagogues, preaching the gospel of the kingdom, and healing every sickness and every disease among the people. But when He saw the multitudes, He was moved with compassion for them, because they were weary and scattered, like sheep having no shepherd. Then He said to His disciples, "The harvest truly is plentiful, but the laborers are few. Therefore pray the Lord of the harvest to send out laborers into His harvest."
>
> — Matthew 9:35–38

It was years later, and eventually, I finally experienced my breakthrough in 2021. I finally realized that my rebellion was not against the church but against Satan working through it.

I moved to North Carolina and temporarily stayed with a godly woman named Faith. Initially, I planned on looking for a home in Florida but could not find one. So, I laid out one specific request before the Lord. I wanted a place with a palm tree. A friend told me to move into an apartment before buying a home. I received her wise counsel. After much research and prayer in looking for a place to live, I stumbled across apartment information in Florida, but it was filled. I then glanced at the bottom of the company website page offering apartment rentals in various cities. The first city that caught my eye was Houston. In the back of my mind, I thought living in Houston and attending a globally known church would be nice, but I wanted to live the rest of my life in Florida. So, I thought, *What am I doing on this page? Go back and keep looking around in Florida.*

But my finger clicked on "Houston," and several results showed that apartments were available. I liked what I saw on the website even though I had never seen the apartment physically. So, in blind faith, I called the manager and put down the deposit.

A few weeks later, I left North Carolina and drove to Texas with a U-Haul trailer hitched to the back of my SUV. I arrived at 3:30 a.m. but could not move into my apartment until later that morning. As I drove around in the dark to find rest, a humungous billboard sign with display lights over the huge words read, "You Can Find Grace Here." I cried and knew that I was where God wanted me to be. I drove over to where the sign stood near that church. I parked on their property, and the dogs and I went fast asleep. Deep inside, I knew I was under a waterfall of God's amazing grace.

Later that morning, I checked in with the apartment manager to begin the move-in process. I entered my apartment with my dogs. Everything was so beautiful inside. Then I stepped out onto my patio, and behold, a colossal palm tree stood there. I cried with tears of joy and thanked God for answering my prayer. Its vast leaves shaded my patio. It was so tall and beautiful to behold.

Walking my dogs around the property, I noticed seven other humongous palm trees surrounding the swimming pool. As my dogs went on a smell tour of every inch of the property, I saw no other palm trees at the apartment buildings except mine. My apartment was the only dwelling that had a palm tree. When I mentioned it to my leasing manager, she said my apartment was the *crème de la crème*.

The Holy Spirit recalled in my mind from the book of Psalms,

> O Lord, how great are Your works!
> Your thoughts are very deep.
> A senseless man does not know,
> Nor does a fool understand this.
> When the wicked spring up like grass,
> And when all the workers of iniquity flourish,
> *It is* that they may be destroyed forever.
> But You, Lord, *are* on high forevermore.
> For behold, Your enemies, O Lord,
> For behold, Your enemies shall perish;

All the workers of iniquity shall be scattered.
But my horn You have exalted like a wild ox;
I have been anointed with fresh oil.
My eye also has seen *my desire* on my enemies;
My ears hear *my desire* on the wicked
Who rise up against me.
The righteous shall flourish like a palm tree,
He shall grow like a cedar in Lebanon.
Those who are planted in the house of the LORD
Shall flourish in the courts of our God.
They shall still bear fruit in old age;
They shall be fresh and flourishing,
To declare that the LORD is upright;
He is my rock, and *there is* no unrighteousness in
    Him.

                       — Psalm 92:5–15

The palm tree became my memorial stone. God is so good because He knew I needed this as a reminder to help me stand no matter what hits me. Satan had worked overtime through my father in my younger years. After that, Satan continued his destruction in my latter years to steal my joy and my children, even killed my ministry and calling, and destroyed my marriage and family. So, every time I look at the palm tree, it is a reminder from God that I am righteous and that He has me in the "palm" of His hand.

I relate to a palm tree because it can tolerate harsh elements outside. It is a fact that palm trees are the only trees that can survive any tempest, hurricane, cyclone, or even tsunami. When these powerful forces of nature do their violent destruction, the palm tree will flex or bend over, but it will never uproot from the ground. This is because the palm tree has a unique root system. No force can pull the palm tree out of the earth. It will stay bent no matter what hits it. It takes all the beatings, whiplashes, and everything that comes against it. After the intemperate storm has passed, the palm tree will not stay bent. Instead, it will stand back up to its original position. It may need nutrients and care to heal, but it will remain standing.

Throughout my childhood, I had survived my father's harsh and cruel abuse, yet deep down inside me, I was anchored to Jesus.

Romans 8:35–39 says,

> Who shall separate us from the love of Christ?
> Shall tribulation, or distress, or persecution, or
> famine, or nakedness, or peril, or sword? As it is
> written: "For Your sake we are killed all day long;
> We are accounted as sheep for the slaughter." Yet
> in all these things we are more than conquerors
> through Him who loved us. For I am persuaded
> that neither death nor life, nor angels nor princi-
> palities nor powers, nor things present nor things
> to come, nor height nor depth, nor any other cre-
> ated thing, shall be able to separate us from the
> love of God which is in Christ Jesus our Lord.
>
> — Romans 8:35–39

DISCLAIMER:

This Is A True Story.

The sexual abuse depicted by my father lasted almost daily for eleven consecutive years. Adult discretion is advised.

I do not intend to hurt any person, whether they are deaf or hearing, of a different nationality, sex, race, community, sect, or religion. However, please understand that everything that happened in my childhood was beyond and out of my control. Everything that my father did, I opposed. What he did was wrong and unjust to me, the family, and everyone he knew.

Most of the names of the survivors and the dead have been changed for privacy purposes.

I am just an ordinary person who wrote this book.

I am doing it for that little girl.

I am doing it for Thelma.

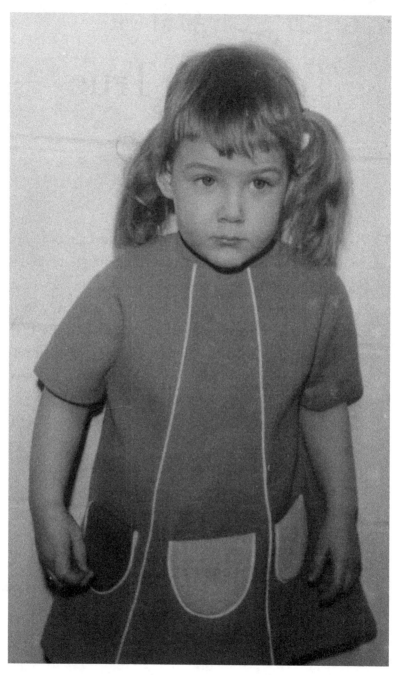

The author at two-and-a-half years old.

Unheard Screams | Morgan Critzer

TABLE OF CONTENTS

Dedication iii
Acknowledgments v
Introduction ix
Disclaimer: This Is A True Story.. xxiii

Prologue 27

Chapter One: Illegitimate Disaster 31
Chapter Two: The Altar of Child Sacrifice 39
Chapter Three: In the Middle of Nowhere 49
Chapter Four: Sweet Music and Candy 57
Chapter Five: Home Away from Home 71
Chapter Six: One Step Forward and Two Steps Back . . . 87
Chapter Seven: Living on the Boundary Lines 93
Chapter Eight: Steal, Kill, and Destroy 99
Chapter Nine: Taking Hysteria Out of Hysterectomy . . 111
Chapter Ten: Survival Mode 121
Chapter Eleven: Earth, Wind, and Fire 131
Chapter Twelve: Sold and Carried Away 139
Chapter Thirteen: The Night Jesus Knocked at the Door 147
Chapter Fourteen: Sweet and Sour Sixteen 153
Chapter Fifteen: A Father's Love for a Fatherless Father 167

Epilogue 181
Afterword: Grace, Grace to It 185

PROLOGUE

It was my second year at Asbury College (a.k.a. Asbury University). I was twenty-two years old. Toward the end of the first semester, most college students had plans to travel back home for the holidays. However, I stumbled across a sign-up sheet on the college boards with an opportunity to ring bells with the iconic red kettle for the Salvation Army. This sounded like a fantastic idea for students like me who had nowhere to spend the holidays. After all, their motto, "Doing the Most Good," was what Christmas was all about.

There were many major cities, like Boston and Pittsburg, but I chose Miami. It was the farthest and warmest destination of the choices listed. About a dozen of us students signed up to go there. The college paid for the airfare and hotel accommodation.

When we arrived, we stayed at a five-star hotel. I shared a room with a fellow student named Christy. Our room was very spacious. The plan was to stay there for about a month.

Early the following day, we registered and attended a meeting. While there, I observed low-income and struggling families standing in line at a nearby warehouse to receive necessities.

We met with our prominent Salvation Army leader. He was Haitian and spoke broken English. He wore a decorated military-like uniform, which I learned was the Salvation Army protocol. The leader split us up individually to work at targeted malls, while only a few worked together inside the malls for the Salvation Army Angel Tree program. He drove a huge white shuttle van and dropped us off at our designated posts. Also, he set up a red kettle along with the bell for each person. I worked outside, farther away from the mall entrance.

Each day was the same setup and routine. I worked full-time shifts as I rang the bell and greeted "Merry Christmas" to the shoppers who dropped money donations into the kettle.

Our group headed back to the hotel. We swam at the pool and hung out together under the beautiful Miami sun.

One day, the leader arrived unusually early, picked me up and a few other students, and dropped us off at the hotel. The others were still working. By then, I was famished. I headed directly to a restaurant that was located inside the hotel. I sat alone, studied the menu for a long time, and ordered food.

After the waitress delivered my meal, a man suddenly yelled, "Hey, come over here and eat with us!" I looked over at where the voice was coming from and saw three people. Two men and a woman. They appeared to be middle-aged. I scanned my surroundings and looked back at those people at the table. The man was looking straight at me. I pointed my finger at myself and said, "Are you talking to me?" He replied in a friendly and upbeat voice, "Yes, bring your food over and sit with us." I suspiciously hesitated for a second, but then I accepted his offer.

The man introduced himself and his friends. He shared that they all worked together at the financial building adjacent to the hotel. I learned that they were stockbrokers. I quickly nodded and said, "Hi," as I glanced at the other man beside him. Then I turned my head left and greeted the lady who sat opposite me at the end of the table. They did not seem very friendly or sociable.

After a few minutes of small talk, the man asked me what I was doing in Miami. I shared with him that I was with students from Asbury College in Kentucky. I also added that we were reaching out to help those in need through the Salvation Army.

He piped up super loud and enthusiastically asked me, "Are you a Christian?" I replied, "Yes," with a nod. He laughed a belly ache laugh, causing a scene in the restaurant. I did not know why that would be so funny.

Then, pointing to each person sitting at the table, he said, "You are a Christian, I am a Catholic, this guy is a Jew, and she is an Atheist." He continued his belly laugh. I thought it was bizarre and comedic after he pointed that out. The other two did not show any response to his comment. It appeared that they were used to his antics. I looked at him and snickered at what he said. I momentarily contemplated that this was like a scene from a movie.

The Catholic immediately shot me with a question, asking me to share with him my story and why I became a Christian. No one had ever asked me that question before. He put me on the spot. I took a deep breath to calm my nerves and then shared my testimony for the first time.

CHAPTER ONE:

Illegitimate Disaster

"We have to get married immediately!" exclaimed my mother in sign language. "I do not want my family to know that I am pregnant. We must keep this a secret!" Wild-eyed and desperate to cover her shame, she pressured my fifty-five-year-old deaf father to marry her immediately. My father felt it was finely suited since my mother was blonde, pretty, and twenty years younger than him. But, married or not, he would continue to live footloose and fancy-free, fulfilling his fleshly lusts.

My father had a bad reputation. Everywhere he went, he stirred up trouble. He was a tall, muscular, and broad-shouldered man standing six feet, three inches tall. He had tattoos on both sides of his arms. The one side of his arm portrayed strange images and inscribed "KKK." At twelve years of age, he left school. At a young age, he became an alcoholic, chewed tobacco, and drank a dozen cups of straight black coffee daily. He joined the second legion of the Ku Klux Klan in Chicago around 1925 until it dissolved. He bragged about his murders in the past, for which, unfortunately, he had never been caught.

My father was the only one on his side of the family who was deaf. In 1913, his biological father abandoned him and his mother, Lucy. They were never married. My father could hear and speak before he lost his hearing.

Within a year, his mother married another man named William.

Father grew up in his formative years with his mother, stepfather, and younger stepbrother, Harry, whose nickname was "Rocky."

In 1917, his stepfather attempted suicide. He was taken to the medical hospital for treatment and stayed overnight. Nothing would stop him. He tried again, this time by jumping out of the hospital window. Since both suicide attempts failed, he caught pneumonia at the hospital and died within two weeks.

Another tragedy happened while Grandmother Lucy was still in mourning. A Spanish flu plague swept through Chicago in 1918. My father caught the flu and also suffered spinal meningitis, a disease that caused the loss of my father's hearing in both ears.

Later in life, as a young adult, he became a violent and angry man. Everyone had to tread carefully around him. Alcoholism, gambling, and sex dominated his life. He was the ringleader in the deaf community and hosted beer and poker parties almost every weekend. At one of those parties, my father volunteered to grill hamburgers. After the meal, he got everyone's attention and, in sign language, thanked everyone for the compliments. Then, he shared with them his secret recipe. He worked everyone up by going into great detail about each ingredient in the hamburgers. Finally, when he mentioned canned dog food as the final ingredient, immediately, some of the deaf people gagged, and one person threw up. Others rose in anger and left. Some of his drunk friends mentioned that it tasted delicious. Despite this prank, my father had no regard for anyone's feelings.

My father's side of the family he grew up with could all speak and had busy, successful lives. He was intentionally left out of the main family event gatherings because he was deaf, illegitimate, and from another father. As unbelievable as it may seem, he never knew he was illegitimate, but his mother and stepbrother did. His mother falsely legalized his last name, which belonged to his stepfather. My father had believed that Harry and he were blood brothers from the same father and mother. My father and his half-siblings were from four different fathers. There were no similarities between him and his siblings. Growing up with them was a challenge as his family had to learn sign language to communicate with him. His French half-brother Harry was a successful man in his own right. He was married and had a son and daughter. Both went to the Navy and Air Force. Uncle Harry spent most of his time with his antique automobile collection of Studebakers. His half-sister, Lilly, owned a retail store in Chicago. He had two other Italian half-siblings, Irene and Elmer, also known as "Buster," who were successful, too. These were hard for my father to see and process since he could not give out the exact measure of success as them because of his deaf impairment that limited him. My father's rejection and hopelessness pent up, giving way to bitterness that led to explosions of angry outbursts, sexual immorality, and severe alcohol addiction.

My mother's announcement of her hasty marriage to my father did not garner any support. My mother's parents, Gerry and Pearl, and her siblings, Alice and John, did everything they could to stop her from marrying my father. They meant well, but she was stuck with the little secret inside her belly. She felt trapped in the scandal, with her family on one side and my father on the other.

It was only a matter of days in March 1968 before my father and mother tied the knot through the justice of the peace. Mother moved in with Father in his Chicago home, but it was short-lived. She did not like the city and wanted to return to live close to her family. So, they eventually moved and bought a house on Homer Avenue, a few miles from my grandparent's home in Elkhart, Indiana. Unfortunately, the marriage to my father caused a rift between her and her family. They preferred that my mother and father stay far away.

My grandparents, Aunt Alice, and Uncle John, were afraid of my father. They were gentle and peaceful people by nature. During visits, Grandpa Gerry retreated to his bedroom with his black terrier and locked the door. He was the only one in the family that could hear and speak. Grandma Pearl was deaf. She often sat on her reclining chair. The television volume was turned up high so Grandpa Gerry could listen from his bedroom. My grandmother's side of the family was all genetically deaf from an inherited rare genetic condition called Waardenburg syndrome. The symptoms of this syndrome are hearing loss and pigmentation of the skin, which, in their case, was pale white skin. Their eyes were affected, too. A few family members had lazy eyes and had to wear glasses with a powerful prescription. Another was an unusual characteristic patch or streak of white hair in the middle front of their forehead. By their mid-thirties, their hair would turn into a natural platinum-white color.

My great-great grandmother Miranda was the first deaf person in the McQueen family known to have inherited the syndrome. An old photo of her revealed a white streak down the middle on top of her head. Therefore, it was passed down from generation to generation, all the way to my mother and her siblings and even to my brother and sister.

Toward the end of October, my mother went to Elkhart General Hospital for her scheduled cesarian. The doctor required her to have a cesarian section because she could not communicate with the doctors and nurses during natural delivery. The C-section did not take long. The nurse whisked me to the hospital nursery as my mother was stitched up for healing and recovery. My mother never nursed me but bottle-fed me with whole milk from cows.

When my father saw me for the first time, he was so happy to know I had his features. He bragged to my mother that I took after him and not her. The biggest question was, could I hear, or was I deaf? My parents were curious to know. The doctor conducted a newborn hearing test, and I passed it with flying colors.

The nurse asked my parents what they would name me to prepare the birth certificate. My father told my mother he would choose my first name since I had most of his features. He remembered a cousin who was like a sister to him as a young teenager. She was considered his closest friend in the family and was always kind to him. Therefore, Thelma became my birth name.

An official birth certificate with a gold seal from Elkhart General Hospital inscribed my birth details. Black ink was slabbed on the bottom of my feet and imprinted on the back of the certificate along with my mother's thumbprints. The nurse swaddled me back into my blanket, hiding my black-stained feet. Finally, she gave the birth certificate to my parents. They could not hear how my name, "Thelma Therrien," was read on the birth certificate. It did not make any difference to them, but it would someday hugely affect me.

After our hospital stay for a few days, my parents and I finally went home. My mother's family members did not welcome me because they figured out the timing of my birth and labeled me illegitimate.

They also regarded me as identical to my father because they believed his bad blood ran through my veins. My grandparents treated me as a curse. They despised and rejected me. Even though my grandpa Gerry could speak, he never looked or said one word to me during his lifetime. Grandma Pearl was polite and kind but not affectionate toward me. She showed favoritism to my aunt Alice's children.

*My father was holding me on my first day at home
right after my birth from the hospital.*

CHAPTER TWO:

The Altar of Child Sacrifice

A couple of years later, when I was two and a half years old, my mother brought me and my one-year-old fraternal twin brother and sister into my father's bedroom. I had never been inside of it. It had a queen-sized bed with a silver satin comforter on it. The curtains were closed. The atmosphere was very dark, and the air felt cold. A lamp was on, yet it seemed like the light could not penetrate the bedroom's darkness. A chill immediately swept over me, and I retaliated against my mother and wanted to leave. But instead, she reprimanded me in sign language to stand still and not move.

I watched her pull my sister's pants down to her ankles. I could not help but see my sister's nakedness. My mother lifted her and laid her on my father's bed. She told her to lay still. My conscience as a toddler alerted me that this would not be good.

Next, my mother unbuttoned my brother's pants and pulled them to his ankles. That was the first time I had seen a boy's privates. I was surprised and afraid of what my mother was doing. I watched my mother lift my brother and lay him beside my sister on the bed. She told them to lay still and stop fidgeting. I watched my siblings lying on the bed with their privates exposed. I felt vulnerable and unsafe, knowing that I was next.

Immediately, my mother approached me and reached her hands to pull my pants down. I retreated and threw a tantrum. With force, she grabbed my shoulder, pulled me toward her, and pointed her finger at me, signing me to stand still and not move. She pulled my pants down, which puddled around my ankles. I could not walk or run away from my mother. The half-worn pants stuck around my ankles were substituted as a chain. I immediately felt the chilly air in the room on my body. I wanted my pants back on. Everything happened so fast that I realized I was lying beside my brother and sister. We were laid across perfectly, touching shoulder to shoulder like a can of sardines. We all wore our shirts; only our privates were exposed together on my father's bed.

I froze with fear of what was going to happen next. I was alert to every detail that was happening.

My mother told us repeatedly to lay still and not move. She placed her pointer finger to her mouth and then left the bedroom.

I looked over at my brother and sister; they looked up at the ceiling, unaware of what was happening. Like any other time, they probably thought they were getting their diapers changed. I knew that we were not getting diaper changes. This was different. A sick sensation swept throughout my mind, and chill bumps appeared on my body from the cool temperature in the room.

A couple of minutes later, my mother took the lead, holding my father's hand. They entered through the door into his bedroom. In sign language, she told him she had a surprise for him. She was excited and could not wait to show off her surprise. She gestured to my father to look at his bed and pointed her finger at our nakedness. Their eyes were gazing at us. My mother was laughing and gesturing in sign language about how small and cute our private parts were. My father was not laughing while processing my mother's surprise for him. His eyes glanced across our naked bodies and were then fixed on mine. Without realizing it, my mother opened the door of spiritual incest. My father's bed became an altar of child sacrifice.

On a hot summer day, I recall watching my favorite morning programs: *Sesame Street*, *Captain Kangaroo*, and *Mister Rogers' Neighborhood*. Since my parents could not speak or even read books verbally to me, my mother turned on these programs daily as my substitute babysitter. I was excited every time Big Bird appeared on *Sesame Street*.

She placed my playpen far away from the black and white television set with the volume on high, yet close enough to the kitchen to keep her eyes on me while she worked.

After my lunch, it was time for my daily afternoon nap. My bedroom walls had a cheerful sunshine yellow color. My mother laid me down, pulled the white bed sheet over me, and closed the door.

I was peacefully asleep with my back on the bed when suddenly, I was stirred by something moving and touching inside me. With my head on the pillow facing the ceiling, my eyes fluttered, and my senses were awakened from my deep sleep. I opened my eyes and turned to the right to see my father's face about an inch away from mine. I shrieked as if I had seen a monster. He smiled at me as if everything was okay. I turned my head away from his and looked the opposite way. My body froze, and I was paralyzed with fear. He was lying beside me with the white bed sheet covered over us. What he was doing to me while smiling simultaneously did not make sense. I could not move. I felt his giant hand, long fingers, and sharp claw-like nails inside me. It hurt me very much, and I felt a burning sensation. I did not look at my father. I lay on my back like a corpse, stared at the ceiling, and showed no emotion.

Immediately, my mother walked into the bedroom. I saw her face pale when she saw my father lying on my bed. He could not hear her while he sexually abused me. She quickly grabbed the bed sheet and screamed in horror when she saw his hand inside my underwear. My father bolted straight up after being caught red-handed with blood on his fingers. He violently threatened to kill her if she told anyone. My mother yielded to his threat. Fear gripped my mother and me from that day forward.

I got up and sat on my bed to look down curiously at where my father was touching and discovered a large amount of blood between my legs and on the bed sheets. I knew that seeing blood was not a good sign. My virginity was stolen and destroyed. After my father hastily left my bedroom, my mother stripped my bed of the blood-stained clothes and bed sheets and soaked them in a bucket with laundry soap and cold water. She kept it in there till our next trip to the laundromat. From that day forward, I slept with my mother on her bed. So, if anything ever happened, I could warn her. My baby brother and sister's crib were also moved into the bedroom with us. So, all of us were together in the same room while my father was alone in his bedroom.

As a CODA (Child of Deaf Adults), I did not have opportunities like normal children who could hear and speak. Besides the blaring television, silence dominated the home. I grew up in my formative years communicating only with my hands. I learned to communicate with the deaf using sign language, facial expressions, and body language. I had to use my eyes to process the communication instead of my ears.

When I was growing up, my family communicated with an old Welsh English version of sign language. Although many signs were similar, it was not ASL (American Sign Language). My father attended the Ephpheta School for the Deaf in Chicago, which Catholic priests and nuns managed and supervised in the late 1910s and 1920s. He left and returned many times until he finally quit early in eighth grade.

My mother and her siblings attended the Indianapolis School for the Deaf. They boarded at the school for most of their childhood and teenage years. Therefore, my deaf parents did not see their families except during holidays and summer breaks. My mother completed her requirements and graduated from the deaf school.

Since my parents could not speak my name, "Thelma," they had their versions. My mother would make a high-pitched, shrill voice to get my attention. That was my name. Father had a deep voice and spoke with a guttural sound, "Uh-dub-duh." That was my name, too.

My family could not control their vocal sound levels when they uttered them unknowingly. Sometimes, it was loud, and sometimes not. They breathed heavily, not knowing how it sounded to others who could hear. As a child, I adopted their behaviors. Therefore, I had no control over how loudly I spoke. When I talked to hearing people, I unconsciously moved my hands and arms as if gesturing in sign language.

Another way my deaf family communicated in the home was by stomping on the floor. It created vibrations so that we could feel it. We also threw objects across the room. Normal means was by tapping on the shoulder.

———————

Going to bed every night had been tough. Fear of darkness grappled me. Panic and anxiety were my constant companions.

I fought hard not to sleep at night because I had the same consistent nightmares. The details were vivid in my mind. It felt so real. I saw myself falling into a deep, dark, endless abyss. I screamed as I felt my body drop at a fast speed. The hole had no bottom. The momentum of my fall caused me to wake up screaming. My hair and whole body were soaking wet every time I had that nightmare.

I sat up and looked around to see where I was at. I looked to the right side to see my mother sleeping close to the edge of the bed. She lay peacefully still. I turned my head toward the left of the bedroom and saw my siblings asleep in their crib. I then looked at the bedroom door. It was shut. I returned to bed and covered my head with a blanket to hide from this darkness that wanted my soul.

My sister, Dottie, was born with crippled legs and had surgery to correct them. She had to see a doctor often for checkups. I looked forward to going to the doctor's office because the waiting room had a table filled with Uncle Arthur's *Bible Stories* hardcover books. Even though I could not read, the pictures were colorful and depictive enough for me to understand the Bible. I wanted to enter the pages of the book and meet this Jesus.

One day, three strangers came to our home. It was a woman and her two children. My mother let them in. They were kind and looked like a happy family. The children were older than me. One was a boy with glasses, and the other was a girl with long blonde hair. The woman did not know sign language, so my mother hurriedly brought out a notebook pad and blue pen to communicate with her. My mother always kept a notebook on hand, just in case. They wrote notes back and forth for a while. Finally, the woman asked my mother if she wanted to attend church with her. She said I could attend a children's church, and there was a nursery available for my siblings. Of course, my mother accepted her invitation.

That first Sunday morning, the woman came by to pick us up for church. I recall my mother changing my brother and sister's diapers on the hardwood floor while my father stood and looked on as we got ready. He was on high alert, assessing the whole situation. Before we left, he reminded my mother that he would kill her if she tattled about him to the stranger or anyone at church. My mother's face showed fear. I quickly looked away from his threats and looked at the stranger. The stranger had no idea what my father said but smiled gracefully and pleasantly at him. Mother finally got my brother and sister ready. She packed up the diaper bag and could not wait to leave the house, nor could I.

Since then, going to church with them every Sunday was like going to a haven. I remember my excitement every Sunday when the woman and her children came and knocked at the front door. Their warm smiles cheered me. I often went to church with them without my mother. She was constantly stressed out and opted to stay home most of the time because of taking care of the twins.

At Sunday school, I sat at a round white table with black and white chairs with other children my age. A male teenage volunteer shared a Bible story. I sat there soaking it all in, like when I watched Big Bird tell stories on *Sesame Street*. After the story, he passed blank white sheets of paper around the table and asked us to draw a picture of Jesus. With my paper and crayons, I remember drawing a big circle of Jesus's face. I drew eyes and a pleasant smile and added wavy hair on His head. I felt an instant connection. There was something about Jesus that I wanted so desperately. I was so excited and proud of my drawing that I could not wait to show my mother.

After the strangers dropped me off at home, I proudly showed my mother my drawing. She glanced at it without any reply and then quickly turned around and walked away. Her cold response stung my heart.

Later, I looked everywhere for my drawing and asked my mother where it was. Again, she just shrugged her shoulders and did not respond.

I could not find Jesus anywhere. It bothered me that I could not locate it. My missing drawing of Jesus was the deciding factor to follow Him just like the strangers did. Their God became my God.

This photo was taken at the three strangers' house when I was two and a half years old. Her son and daughter are pictured on the wall.

Chapter Two: The Altar of Child Sacrifice   47

CHAPTER THREE:

In the Middle of Nowhere

The summer of 1973 ended, and the early fall took its place. I was almost five years old at the time. My mother dressed me and did my hair in piggy tails. Then she rushed me to eat a bowl of bland oatmeal with milk. When I finished eating, my father groaned my name and gestured for me to go outside with him. He took my left hand after we exited the house. We walked on the sidewalk on Homer Avenue toward Hively. I did not know where we were walking, but I enjoyed this new adventure. As we approached the intersection, he signed to me that I must stop there before crossing the road. He pointed to many cars whizzing by us and said that if I walked in front of a car, I would get hit and die. He demonstrated how I should look on the left and right sides of the road before crossing it. Once it was clear, we hustled to the other side.

After we crossed, my father pointed his finger at a speed limit signpost. When I saw it, he told me it should be my landmark to turn left. So, we walked down the sidewalk and past a street. We kept going till we approached another road. We turned right on it and headed toward an elementary school on the left side.

We walked up to a fence that was on the school property. Many children were playing outside on the playground. Father gestured for me to go on ahead. He said that when I finished school, he would be waiting for me in the same spot where he was standing. I looked at him, looked at the children, and looked at him again. Finally, he pointed me to go, so I obediently started walking toward the group of children and stopped in the middle of the playground. I stood there alone, not knowing a soul. Everything swirled around me, with loud children playing and adults chatting away. I had never witnessed so many children in real life. I looked back to find my father and saw him walking toward home.

A young woman approached me and asked if my name was Thelma. I nodded my head with a "yes." She gently took my hand and said, "Come with me." She led me inside the school to my kindergarten class. She dropped me off, and I gazed all around the giant classroom.

The teacher was old with curly gray hair. She was an unsympathetic, unbending, and matter-of-fact woman. She managed her classroom strictly and in a very orderly fashion. I could not understand most of what the teacher was blathering about during class. I was not used to being around people that talked. I was only used to being around deaf people. I felt out of place. I was dazed by their speech and by how fast they were talking. Students would talk to me, but I could only formulate a couple of words out of my mouth, and if I did not understand, I just blankly stared at them. During our seatwork, I looked around at my classmate's assignments and copied them. That was all I knew to do.

After school, I ran across the playground and saw my father standing outside the fence line entrance. I met up with him, and we walked back home together.

When we arrived home, my father took my school clothes off. Then he lifted me to sit on the bathroom counter. He served me a jar of different flavored suckers. I grabbed one, opened the wrapper, and put it in my mouth. He put his finger inside me. I was confused and afraid, but his deceit and manipulation by using candy worked. Of course, all I wanted was candy. He told me that he loved me, which sent mixed signals in my mind. I knew deep down that was not true. Because I knew that my father had outbursts of anger and was violent, I complied with his demands and did everything I could to please him.

I followed my father to the kitchen and saw him put the candy jar away inside the cabinet above the refrigerator. It was high and out of reach.

My father continually walked me to school and back home for about a week. I looked forward to seeing him after school, standing at the fence waiting for me. I ran excitedly to him and could not wait to show him my classwork. I enjoyed our walks together even though I had a lot of mixed feelings about him. I wanted a typical loving father even though he consistently sexually abused me.

It was the following day; my father had gone to work. My mother got me ready and scurried me outside the door. She told me to run along to school, and then she coldly closed and locked the door in my face. After that, I was on my own.

I turned left after I walked down the steps outside the front door. My mind was racing as I tried to remember the route my father had shown me. I walked down Homer toward Hively. I looked both ways and crossed the street carefully as my father instructed me. When I reached the other side, I turned right onto the sidewalk on Hively. I walked the opposite way instead of where I was supposed to go. I was oblivious to my surroundings because I was singing the theme song from *Sesame Street* out loud. As I approached a corner of a busy main street, I turned left on it and observed that there were more cars on this street than where my father showed me. I noticed that there were not any homes. Instead, there were many businesses dotted along the road. I looked down and got distracted by pebbles and ants on the sidewalk when suddenly, the revving speed of so many cars shook me. I scanned my surroundings. It took a while to realize that I did not recognize this road. I was lost. Then, I bawled a loud, piercing cry at the top of my voice. Unfortunately, it was drowned out by the noisy, busy traffic. No one heard my screams.

As bizarre as it may seem, no one stopped to help a five-year-old girl. The world felt like a cruel place. Then, for some reason, I turned around from where I had walked earlier and saw a colossal laundromat sign at the end of the main street and Hively. I recognized it because my mother washed clothes over there frequently. That was the only indicator that helped me find my way back.

With a sigh of relief, I calmed down from my hysterical crying episode. I walked swiftly and did not take my eyes off the sign. It was my crutch of reassurance. As soon as I arrived at the intersection facing the laundromat across the street from me, I looked to my right and recognized the tiny houses in the area. I was able to retrace my steps. Finally, I found the speeding signpost my father told me to remember. I stood next to it, looked around, and saw the street where I lived. I then started walking the other way on Hively.

Finally, I arrived late to school all in one piece. The students were sitting on the large area rug playing. I sat on the floor with them. Immediately, a boy grabbed me and pulled me to sit beside him. He held me tight and told me to stay and not move. Then, he put his hands inside my underwear. I began to think and wonder if this was what fathers and boys always did to girls. After that, the boy targeted me at every chance he could get. I was not too fond of his brazen advances. I stared at my teacher, hoping she would see what was happening. I was too afraid to ask her for help.

After several weeks, I became well-versed in my route of walking to and back from school. On my way home one day, I was a few hundred feet away from approaching my house when three boys started running toward me. They looked like they were in third grade. They were shouting and laughing and running super-fast. I panicked and charged toward my house. I grabbed the door handle to open it, but it was bolted and locked. I screamed and pounded on the door.

Mother could not hear. Breathlessly, I pounded on the front door, hoping she could feel the vibrations. My strength as a five-year-old was compared to a light knock. I looked back, hoping the boys would not get close enough to hurt me. The boys laughed and ran past my house. I was deeply relieved they left me alone. Although, I was not glad when my mother locked me outside the house for about half an hour. I walked toward the living room window, but the curtains were closed. I did not know what to do except stand there and wait at the front doorstep.

Looking back, I believe the boys did not set out to hurt me. However, I thought in my mind that they would hurt me because that was all I ever learned from my father. My father's abuse created a domino effect in all my human relationships, and worse was that I was treated as if I had value.

Mother finally opened the door to let me in. I signed to her that I had waited outside for a long time, but nothing seemed to phase her. She did not act concerned for me or asked me how school went.

There was a disconnect between my mother and me. I sensed it early on as a child. She spent little time with me except when she needed me. Although, there was one time she showed me old family photos. She went into detail about the names and dates as if she was reliving her past life of the good memories she had with her family.

Another way my mother showed love was when she held my hand every night at bedtime. She held it tightly as if she was the one who needed love the most. I let her hold it because I needed affection, too, knowing we were in the same boat together. We did not know if we were going to sink or swim.

Many times, I observed her signing to herself in sign language. For my mother, being unable to hear and speak to anyone outside her created another world in her mind. My mother was held hostage. My father isolated her and did not let her have friends because of fear that she would reveal his dark and terrible sins. She was only allowed to see her family members and a few deaf people that both my parents associated with. If she needed to associate with anyone else, he would remind her of the severe consequence of death if she tattled on him. My father's constant fearmongering caused our minds to be entangled with anxiety. I had severe panic attacks and breathing problems because of my father.

Existing as a CODA and being abused sexually was complex, leaving me confused. I had no choice but to learn to adjust to that way of life. It was not their fault that they were deaf. I was stuck in the middle. Even though I was not deaf, I still could not adjust in my kindergarten class with everyone who could hear and speak. My teacher did not mediate to help guide and merge me into the hearing culture.

I was alone and did not belong to either side. I felt lost in the middle of nowhere.

CHAPTER FOUR:

Sweet Music and Candy

I waved my paperwork during class to get my teacher's attention because I needed help, so I said aloud, "Teacher!" She did not respond. So, I enunciated her name slowly again with a louder pitch than before, "Teeeacher!"

The scowl on her face matched her shout that resounded with irritation. She retorted, "My name is not Teacher! My name is Ms. Skinner!" Her response made me wish I could vanish into thin air. I felt humiliated. The class froze instantly into a dead silence. I thought saying "Teacher" was an appropriate way to address her. I did not know she had another name.

I wanted to return home to watch *Sesame Street* and listen to Big Bird's bright and bubbly voice on TV. He was much more lovable than my teacher. I was curious to learn, but she never talked to me or assisted me in understanding anything. Instead, she was stern and implacable toward me. There were some students whom she favored in class. But, deep down, she made me believe I did not belong there.

After our naptime, she called everyone over to form together into a circle. She told all of us to count from one to ten individually. As each boy and girl took turns going slowly around the circle, I listened to each student recite the numbers without making a mistake. Nobody had taught me to count to ten, but I could count to three. I felt my eyes widen, and dread overtook me. Finally, it was almost my turn. I tried hard to remember the number order as each student counted, but my nerves got the best of me. I feared my teacher and imagined her yelling and shaming me again. Finally, when it was my turn, I looked at her and instantly bawled at the top of my voice. That was my last day of school.

After one month of adversity at the public elementary school, I transferred to another school at a special ed class my deaf brother and sister attended. I went there for the remainder of the school year. It was a small class with deaf students. I got along more with them than with the hearing children at my former public school because the deaf culture was all I knew. I could not form words together into sentences to speak and communicate well, but I could communicate comfortably in sign language with all the deaf students.

Two special ed teachers assisted us in the class. They both were incredible and caring people. I received one-on-one attention from them.

Pictured from left to right is my sister Dottie, my brother Ted, and me playing outside at the special ed school.

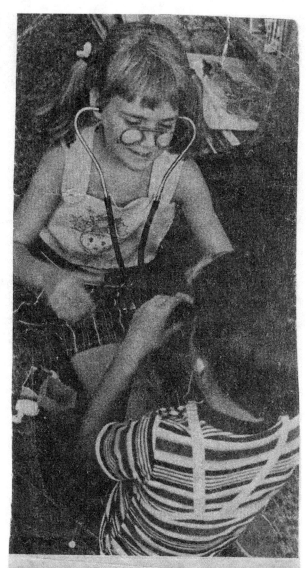

ASSOCIATIVE PLAY occurs when children develop and grow and learn to play in conjunction with others. Thelma Therrien, 5, and Patrick Detwiler, 5, are playing doctor. Although it might look like just fun, the therapeutic value

This 1975 newspaper clipping of me playing doctor with a deaf classmate wearing hearing aids in special ed class.

I had so much fun in that class that one of the teachers brought out all the ingredients and kitchen tools needed to make Christmas sugar cookies. The best part was spooning the red and green sugar sprinkles and filling them carefully in the centers of the shaped cookie dough.

My father continually sexually abused me several times a week. He bribed and conditioned my mind with candy to control and silence me. The abnormal started to become normal.

My father shaped my mind severely to be fearful of him. It was an obsessive fear to the point that I had trust issues with people and feared what they thought of me. As my father continued to commit incest and hide his dark, secret sins, I was still visited by the three strangers. They faithfully continued to take my brother, sister, and me to church.

As a child, I had a keen awareness deep down inside me of a dark evil lurking around my life. I wanted it to go away. Trauma was one of the paralyzing recipes of disaster that gained a foothold in my mind. My father and mother opened doors for many dark spirits to claim their rights over me by forming strongholds in my mind throughout the years. Yet, on the other hand, there was this Jesus whom I had been learning about from my Sunday school teacher, who read a parable that Jesus taught in the book of Matthew 18:10–14. It was about a shepherd leaving the ninety-nine sheep to rescue the one lost from the sheepfold. In my mind, I pictured Jesus as the Shepherd who came looking for me and found me.

> Take heed that you do not despise one of these
> little ones, for I say to you that in heaven their
> angels always see the face of My Father who is in
> heaven. For the Son of Man has come to save that
> which was lost. "What do you think? If a man
> has a hundred sheep, and one of them goes astray,
> does he not leave the ninety-nine and go to the

mountains to seek the one that is straying? And if he should find it, assuredly, I say to you, he rejoices more over that *sheep* than over the ninety-nine that did not go astray. Even so it is not the will of your Father who is in heaven that one of these little ones should perish.

— Matthew 18:10–14

Even though I lived in traumatic circumstances, He was always with me in the darkness, guiding my steps even when I did not know it. Jesus was the only one I wanted to follow and be with. If it were not for the three strangers, I would not have had any hope from all the afflictions I had to trudge through.

Dottie, me, and Ted at Sunday school are pictured from left to right.

Chapter Four: Sweet Music and Candy   63

During the holiday season, my father and I went to the mall. I wore my mustard-colored, thick, shaggy winter coat. As soon as we walked in, I was mesmerized by the Christmas song "Sleigh Ride" performed by the Boston Pops Orchestra. It sounded like a surround sound echoing throughout the mall. I gave a sigh of bliss as the melodic tune tickled my ears. My eyes delighted in the festive sights with myriads of gold ornaments and bright red bows embellished on large green wreaths. An enormous Christmas tree twinkled with red, green, blue, and yellow lights in the middle of the mall, surrounded by fake snow and a red picket fence. Santa Claus sat nearby the tree. Children and parents were lined up to see this jolly character dressed in his red suit. My father and I went and joined in.

When it was my turn to get a photo, I sat on Santa Claus's lap but was not thrilled. All the excitement was so overwhelming to me.

My father ran into one of his friends, Ezra, who worked as a janitor at the mall. He was deaf. He was a lively and outgoing man. They both struck up a conversation in sign language for several minutes until Ezra stopped him and said that he had to get back to work.

My father and I browsed around the mall and entered a music store. He bellowed with a strange groan to get the salesman's attention and gestured to him to help us. Then he pointed at me, then pointed at the record player display, gesturing to the salesman to show me how to operate it. The salesman placed a random LP vinyl record onto the player. I was dumbstruck that sounds came out from this contraption. My father asked me which one I liked. I pointed to a white one. It had a lid that you could close and latch. It also had a portable handle. Father pointed to the salesman, gesturing that he wanted to buy it. We continued shopping, and my father picked out a few Elvis and a dozen different Disney "See, Hear, Read" record albums of *Sleeping Beauty*, *Dumbo*, *The Jungle Book*, and *Pinocchio*, to name just a few.

When we arrived home from the mall, my father set my record player and albums on the living room floor. I sat with my legs crossed for hours and enjoyed listening to the stories and songs on the records.

The end of 1974 was fast approaching. My father drove my mother, siblings, and me to a party. It was a deaf community gathering that my father hosted to ring in the new year. There were some people at the party who were CODAs like me. Round tables were everywhere, filled with deaf people playing poker and rummy. On the other side of the room were those playing bingo. Everyone was having a great time. There was a potluck table spread out with food. I lingered with my brother and sister in the snacks and desserts section. People were getting drunk, especially my father, as I watched him flirt with other women throughout the evening. In sign language, he would ask them to have sex with him. Many deaf people, especially my mother, witnessed my father's disgraceful and obscene behavior. Mother typically never said anything lest my father humiliate her in public. She was the kind of person who swept it under the rug and pretended that nothing happened.

As a CODA, it was common at deaf parties to hear no one talking. All I heard was the shuffling of cards, chairs scooting in and out of the tables, and an occasional burp from beer or pop.

During the silence, myriads of fingers, hands, and arms moved erratically in sign language around the room. The one thing deaf people do not have the luxury of is that other deaf people from a distance can see what they are signing about. No matter how near or far deaf people were, I could catch up on the latest news everywhere I turned my head.

Amid the silence was a piano played by someone in another room. A young man played the piano with a light beige suit and a dark tie. He was a CODA. I walked toward him and stood by, listening to him play. I watched his fingers dance everywhere on the piano keys and listened with pure elation to the rhapsodies of the tune. Finally, he looked over and graciously asked me if I wanted to learn how to play. I nodded my head excitedly. He scooted over to one side of the piano seat and kindly let me sit beside him. He played the nursery song "Mary Had a Little Lamb" slowly several times. Then he asked me to copy him while he played the lower octave keys on the piano. We played and sang together in unison until I got the hang of it. He smiled at me and then let me play alone. I played and sang the song repeatedly and pretended to be as accomplished as the young man. Since most people were deaf at the party, I could play for a long time and not bother anyone.

My family and I stayed at the party through the midnight hours. By then, my father was so drunk that he could not walk. There was no way he could drive. One of the CODAs contacted the police to have my father escorted home. When they arrived, I watched the police help my father get into the back of his car. Someone volunteered to drive him home. He staggered so severely that he had to be assisted by several policemen. I panicked from all the drama. Finally, my mother, siblings, and I got into a police car. We were dropped off safe and sound and went straight to bed.

During the night, I woke up suffocating. I could not breathe. I was trapped inside the thick quilted blanket. I reached up with my hands to remove it but could not. I kicked around to get my mother but was stuck and intertwined inside. My mother was too far from me to reach her. She typically slept on the edge of the bed. I screamed, but that never helped. She was not a light sleeper, either. I fought against the quilt, desperate to get out for air. The quilt was so tight around my head that I could not breathe. I was so scared. Squirming and kicking the quilt wadded my body up inside like a ball, which eventually caused me to roll off and fall onto the hardwood floor. My ongoing nightmares produced dramatic episodes such as this. My screams were never heard.

I got up and was finally able to remove the quilt desperately. I quickly inhaled the cool air that filled my lungs. While breathing rapidly, I stood up, looked at my mother, and felt frustrated. She was not there to help me when I needed her, even when she was beside me in the same bed. Finally, I lay back down to bed and softly sang "Mary Had a Little Lamb."

It was the middle of summer, and my mother was in her vegetable garden gathering her harvest. It was the perfect time to get candy without my mother finding out. I looked at the cabinet above the refrigerator where my father hid the candy jar. The task looked impossible, but I was determined to get up there. I wore my *seven days of the week* underwear. It had a specific day labeled on each one. Each day was in different pastel colors. Even though I did not know the days of the week, I wore them alone without any clothes because it was comfortable from the summer heat.

I pulled the dining room chair next to the kitchen counter. I crawled over into the empty sink basin. I stood up and carefully stepped onto the counter. The kitchen cabinets did not have cupboard doors except for the top row. I reached up with my right hand on the top side of the refrigerator while my left hand was holding onto the shelf. With a firm grip, I lifted my left foot onto the bottom shelf, followed by my right foot. I stopped and shuffled my feet slowly on the shelf toward the fridge.

My right hand and elbow rested on the top of it. As my right foot was anchored on the bottom shelf, I moved my left foot onto the second shelf above it. Then, carefully, I reached my left hand onto the top of the refrigerator. I pushed my body up over the fridge with my feet. I finally made it to the top.

I squatted with both feet planted on top of the fridge. Looking down frightened me, but nothing would stop me from getting candy. I listened for any signs of my mother. Finally, I carefully and slowly opened the cabinet halfway and reached my right hand into the candy jar. To my surprise, I saw other kinds of candies. I grabbed a sucker and quickly tore the wrapper off. With the sucker in my mouth, I looked down at the counter. I lay on the top edge of the fridge with my stomach and carefully slithered downward. My skin rubbed and squeaked against the surface of the refrigerator. My toes finally touched the counter while my hands were fastened atop the fridge. I landed safely and proudly completed my candy heist.

Mother returned with a basket filled with vegetables to wash and prepare for a meal. I asked my mother if I could have a piece of the other candy in the cabinet instead of the suckers. She was not quick enough to catch on to how I knew other sweets were on the shelf. She gave me hard butterscotch candy. It was in a beautiful, deep, yellow-colored cellophane wrapper. It was mouthwatering to look at. So, I opened it up without delay and popped it into my mouth with the palm of my hand. It tasted so buttery and sweet. She then gave me a square piece of caramel candy to sample. I concluded that big people's candies tasted better.

CHAPTER FIVE:

Home Away from Home

It was July 1975, and I was six years old. My mother dressed me up in shorts and a matching top. I wore fancy dress shoes with ankle socks. She fussed over my hair, parting it in the middle and making pigtails with my favorite twin bead ponytail holders that looked like they had marbles on them. She combed my bangs for the final touch.

My brother and sister got their fair share of getting ready, too. My mother and father took us outside in the front yard of our home to take pictures of us. It seemed like forever posing for the camera because my brother and sister could not follow directions. Finally, my parents vociferated my name in their usual manner and told me to get my brother and sister's attention. I tapped my brother and sister on their shoulders and pointed my finger for them to look at the camera. Unfortunately, they were distracted by ants.

There was also another problem. The sun was shining directly at us. It was mid-morning, and the sun stood just above my parents. The intense glare from the sun made it difficult to look at them and the camera. Nevertheless, I persisted and tried to get my brother and sister's attention to get this over with.

As my mother and father made a fuss taking our pictures, I was unaware that another chapter in my life was about to be turned. Unbeknownst to me, the photography session turned out to be a farewell session.

A brown Buick LeSabre pulled up on the street in front of our house. A university student with dark brown loose curly hair, deep brown eyes, and a dark tan stepped out of his car. He waved to my parents and spoke to me cheerfully, "Hi, Thelma. It's very nice to meet you. My name is Kevin."

I had never seen this young man before. He was very polite and cordial to all of us and knew minimal sign language. He had a bright white set of teeth and a big smile. My parents gave him a suitcase and other things I recognized that belonged to me. I had no idea why my parents gave him my belongings. As Kevin was putting them inside his car, my father told me it was okay to go with him. Knowing what my father was like, I did not believe him and was unsure if I could trust this stranger. I panicked as my parents hugged me and walked me to Kevin's car on the passenger side. I felt unsettled about the unforesee-able trip as I crawled up to the seat. Kevin buckled me in and closed the door. He shook hands with my father and mother as if a bargain was made. He then waved them goodbye. They waved back at him and waved at me. My mother started to cry. She seemed to be taking it harder than everyone as her face looked very distressed. I gazed at my parents with wide eyes and uncertainty as Kevin started the car and slowly drove down the end of the street.

We headed south to Bloomington, Indiana. Depending on traffic conditions, it was four hours away from my home. Kevin offered me a snack, sitting between us in the middle of the seat. I put my guard up and declined by not responding to him.

The car's dashboard was so high that I could barely see the road. I mostly saw the sky and trees. I periodically would glance at Kevin and turn my head quickly toward my rear window. I did not want him to catch me looking at him. I felt anxious and afraid as the trip seemed to last forever. He asked questions and tried talking to me, but I stubbornly would not say anything.

I stretched my neck and body upward from the passenger seat to look out the window; I did not recognize anything. Everything familiar was gone. I worked myself up into such a frenzy that I threw up on myself and onto the passenger side floor of his car. Kevin's face did not look angry. Instead, he calmly and reassuringly said we would immediately stop somewhere to clean up the vomit. We were on the main highway out in the farm country. It would be a while till we found a rest area or a gas station. I just sat there helplessly, stewing in my vomit. Kevin was calm the whole time.

We finally stopped somewhere to reset. Kevin opened my suitcase and found clean clothes for me to change into. He told me to go to the restroom, take care of my duties, and change into clean clothes. While I was in the bathroom, he cleaned up the vomit and gassed the car. Then, he stood next to his car with a genuine smile. I gave him my soiled clothes, and he placed them into a bag.

We headed back to the car and kept traveling. After a while, I caught myself bobbing my head in different directions while fighting to stay awake. Finally, my body cried out in desperation to lie down to sleep. My head hung down to my chest while the seat belt strapped my body straight back.

After I woke up, Kevin asked, "Are you hungry?" as he pointed his finger at a restaurant nearby. I looked at where he was pointing, and I nodded my head up and down. We went inside and sat at the booth. I was very thirsty. He ordered food for both of us plus 7 Up for my nausea and tummy ache. After a couple of sips, the fizz made me burp. Kevin laughed.

As far as I can recall, we arrived at a boarding school near Indiana University Bloomington. The boarding school looked like a massive mansion on a sloping hill. We entered through the enormous front door. Immediately, the headmistress of the school came out to greet me. She was a short old lady with a massive bouffant of gray wavy hair stacked on her head. Her hair made up for her short height. She welcomed me with a warmhearted smile, "Hi, Thelma. You may call me Ms. Timmons."

There were young adults who lived at the boarding school. They were called "dorm dads" and "dorm moms." The dorm parents supervised the students. Most were university students in the middle of their studies to become teachers. Some were from the university's staff.

One of the dorm moms led me upstairs to my room. The stairs were concrete and painted in light gray paint. She led me to my bedroom, which was near the stairwell. My bedroom had one window with two bunk beds on either side. My bed was on the bottom of the bunk next to the window. I had a nightstand and a dresser that I shared with my bunkmate. The dorm mom helped three other girls and me to settle in our new bedroom. An older girl could barely talk, and the other two, who looked about the same age as me, could scarcely speak.

Various students who attended there were CODAs or had other hearing and speech impairments. There were some students with hearing aids. Children from different walks of life and in varying circumstances attended the boarding school.

After settling in, I had consistent routines every day. My dorm mom brought the girls and me downstairs to a grand playroom. It was humongous. The windows were so high and wide that sunlight beamed through and lit the room. I walked toward the large area rug surrounded by wooden shelves stocked with toys. It consisted of wooden blocks. Some of my favorite toys I remembered were the Tupper Toys Zoo it Yourself Animals and Ants in Your Pants. I liked playing alone and using my creative imagination without interruption. The other boarding school students played alone alongside me, and some played together. I played all the time in the playroom. It was interactive and so much fun. The dorm parents were always kind to us children. They supervised us around the clock and took excellent care of us.

One day, as I was playing, I had to go to the bathroom. I did not want to go, so I kept on playing. I squeezed my bottom and rocked back and forth, trying to hold it but could not. The urine trickled out onto my underwear and pants. I looked around for the dorm parents. I did not want them to know, so I dashed to the restroom across the hall when they were not looking.

I could not pull my pants down when I entered the bathroom stall. I tried to unbutton it, but it seemed impossible. It was too late. I peed so much that it puddled everywhere. I stood there quietly, not wanting anyone to know I was there. It was just me in the bathroom. I could faintly hear everyone in the playroom. I did not know what to do. I stood inside the bathroom stall with my soaked pants, socks, and tennis shoes.

The bathroom door opened. "Thelma?" said the dorm mom. "Yes," I said reluctantly.

Unsure of what would happen next, the dorm mom approached the bathroom stall and asked if I had peed my pants. She already knew I did, but I supposed she wanted me to tell the truth. I told her that I did. She calmly asked me to unlock the stall. I had expected her to yell at me, but she never did. The dorm mom was firm yet patient and kind. She told me to wait so that she could find some clean clothes for me to change into. I stood in the stall waiting. Finally, the bathroom door opened, and another dorm mom with a little girl walked past my stall, slowly looking down at the puddle I created. The little girl commented on the mess. The dorm mom whispered in acknowledgment, leading the little girl to the last bathroom stall, farther away from me.

My dorm mom came back with my dry, clean clothes. She unbuttoned my stubborn button that was tight around my waist and finally took my pants and underwear off. Then, we went near a sink. She washed me down with soap and water and towel-dried me off. She helped me put my clothes on. I wore my favorite funky-colored bell-bottom pants that had patch designs everywhere. Afterward, she told me to go directly to the play area. I ran as fast as possible, and she said, "Stop."

I stopped. She told me that there was no running allowed. I was dismissed and walked as fast as possible to the play area.

Every weekend at the boarding school was an adventure. Our schedule was filled with fun outings. Toward the end of July 1975, on a scorching hot day, all of us children stood in a single file line. I was distracted by my loose tooth and wriggled it. We then started walking with the dorm parents. One took the lead, and the other stood at the end. Some had to assist other students in the middle of the line. We walked down from the boarding school that stood on the hill. The dorm parents taught us safety rules when walking on the sidewalks and crossing the roads. It seemed like a long walk, and we finally arrived at the assembly hall. There were swarms of college students buzzing everywhere in and out of the enormous building. It was so crowded that I stayed with my dorm mom the whole time. We all stood at the entryway, and this gigantic speaker was as big as a monument in front of the building.

The decibel level of the speaker was beyond decry. This specific speaker was far away from the stage. It was wired all the way to the front entrance as it played live music by the rock band Rolling Stones, who entertained in concert that day. It was blaring rock music so loudly that I put my fingers inside my ears. It did not do it justice. It was so overwhelming and deafening that no one could hear what each other was saying. I did not know why we stood at the entrance for a long time, especially in front of the speaker. The music did not seem to faze anyone in my group. I wanted to leave. I pulled on my dorm mom's shirt and covered my ears. Most of the people in our group attended the Rolling Stones concert. Eventually, some of us returned to the boarding school and headed to the playroom. My ears were ringing very severely. As I played, I discovered that my loose tooth was getting looser. The tip of my tongue was pushing it around inside my mouth. It was so loose that it was like hanging on a string.

I saw the resident nurse. She helped remove the tooth and gave it to me. She sent me on my way to my bedroom. I showed it to my dorm mom. She said that if I put my tooth under my pillow, the tooth fairy would leave money under it. I wholeheartedly believed her. I placed my tooth under my pillow and went to sleep. I found a few nickels and dimes under my pillow the following day. I could not believe my eyes. One of my roommates, Angie, and I were the only ones in the bedroom. I showed her what the tooth fairy had brought me. I was so proud of my coins that I kept them under my pillow.

At bedtime, I lifted my pillow, and my coins went missing. I told the dorm mom that my coins had disappeared under the pillow. She helped look for them all over my bedroom. She asked Angie, but she denied it.

The very next morning, the coins reappeared.

———————

I attended the University Elementary School in the fall. One of the dorm parents routinely drove me there every day and picked me up. It was close by. My first-grade teacher was a soft-spoken, pretty lady with blonde hair who wore her hair up with braids intertwined into a bun. She looked Swedish when she wore it that way. I was able to learn confidently because of her.

Weeks passed, and school pictures were coming up. My teacher advised us to wear something nice and ensure our hair was clean and styled. I took her advice to heart.

I chose a yellow shirt because that was my mother's favorite color. My hair was medium-length, and I had bangs. I did not like them, so I decided to fix them. I found a pair of nail clippers on the tray on top of the dresser that belonged to my roommate, Angie. I took chunks of hair underneath the middle area of my bangs and began chipping it up toward my scalp. I looked at the mirror and did not like how it looked, so I chipped it up again. I looked back into the mirror again and was still unhappy with it. I was frustrated at the outcome. Suddenly, the dorm mom walked into the bedroom. I quickly moved my hand behind my back to hide the nail clippers. She looked aghast at the hair clippings on the floor, then looked at me and asked, "What did you do to your bangs?" With a sheepish look, I said nothing and gave her the nail clippers. She inspected the wreckage and said I still had some bangs that helped to conceal the area but that she could not do anything to improve it.

I arrived at school with my yellow shirt and mismatched red and white plaid bell-bottom pants. I did not think about my bangs, nor did anyone comment about them.

The teacher passed plastic index card boxes and four-by-six index cards to each of us during class. I was fascinated by the contraption. Each index card had a tab with a letter from A to Z. We copied each word from the board and wrote it on the index card. Then, we had to figure out the beginning of the word's first letter and file it into the correct file with that same letter.

The teacher told us to stop what we were doing because it was time to get our pictures taken. The photographer took a class picture of us in our classroom and told us to meet in another room after that for individual portraits.

University Elementary School   1975-76   Bloomington, Indiana

We scrambled to the door and stood in a single file. I stood toward the back of the line. We stood there a long time, waiting for the teacher's signal to proceed. After some time, I was out of the line talking with my classmates, and my teacher said, "Thelma, stay back over there." I followed her orders as I turned around and walked all the way back to the end of the line. I was last. All she meant to say was to get back in line, but I misunderstood. When it was time to go, everyone followed the teacher. I stayed at the spot and did not move. Once everyone left the room, I stood there feeling left out and wondered why I could not go with the class to get my picture taken. Maybe it was because I cut my bangs, I thought. Almost twenty minutes had passed, and suddenly, my teacher darted in with a hint of irritation and blurted, "What are you doing here? You're supposed to get your pictures taken." I replied, "You told me to stay back over here."

I am pictured in a hay wagon surrounded by my boarding school dorm parents and dormmates.

On the last weekend of October 1975, the boarding school scheduled a hayride outing. After the escapade, we returned to the boarding school and entered the dining room for a treat. Ms. Timmons and a dorm mom brought out a sheet cake with many candles aglow. It looked incredibly awesome. I had never seen a birthday cake before, nor did I ever have one. I wondered who it was for. Ms. Timmons said it was my and Johnny's birthday cake. Flabbergasted, Johnny and I looked at each other. We did not know we had the same birthday and were seven years old. It was surreal. The cake was all white with the name "Johnny" inscribed in royal blue, and my name, "Thelma," was frosted in a sunny yellow. Everyone sang to the tune of "Happy Birthday," and then Johnny and I blew the candles out together. Ms. Timmons cut the cake into square pieces. The dorm parents helped pass the cake to everyone. It was a delicious, soft, spongy yellow cake with sweet, creamy, buttery frosting. It was the best birthday party I ever had.

I grew and flourished at the boarding school. I also had a tutor who instructed me daily in my speech development. Confidence was built up from the support of my dorm parents and teachers. Besides my studies, being outdoors was vital to my growth. I played outside almost every day. I frequently climbed across the monkey bars, went on the merry-go-round, and played "Red Light, Green Light."

After climbing the monkey bars, I remembered the urge to go to the restroom. So, I jumped down from the play structure and ran inside, but it was occupied.

I stood outside the hallway, waiting for my turn. I was to be next. I got bored, so I pressed my entire body flat against the wall, and then I spread my hands all the way out like a butterfly. The fingers on my right hand were near the part of the door hinges. I was not looking, but my fingers were touching it. The door opened quickly, and a student rushed out to go outside. I felt the door open and then curiously slid my fingers over more when suddenly, I screamed in sheer terror after the door swung back. My three fingers were fastened inside the doorjamb next to the hinges. The dorm mom rushed toward me and opened the door. I shrieked and cried at the top of my voice. She took me to the resident nurse to tend to me. That was the last time I would ever do that again.

One weekend, we loaded onto a yellow school bus and traveled south of Indiana near Kentucky to explore a cave. All the dorm parents went, too. When we arrived outside the cave entrance, one of the dorm dads went over the rules as if we were in a military regiment. He spoke in a clear, thunderous voice. Each dorm parent was assigned specific students to look after and was given a flashlight.

We entered the cave. It was pitch black before us. I held hands with one of the girls and followed my dorm mom in front of me. In a single file, we hiked through the rocky cavern. My tennis shoes submerged into the puddles of water spots everywhere along the footpath. Ultimately, the soaked squishing sounds echoed in the hollow cavern. The dorm parents would warn us of what was ahead and to be careful. As we got farther in, the cave got narrower. We had to hunch over and duck our heads down; at other times, we crawled on our knees through small passages. One boy yelled out to watch for bats. This did not make the hike fun, believing bats were in the cave. Noises and echoes were constant throughout. I began to feel phobic and wanted to get out of this confinement.

I felt relieved when there was light at the end of the tunnel. We trudged carefully to avoid the protrusions of the rocks in the cave overhead. Just before we exited the tunnel, there was one more sizeable muddy water spot we had to cross through to leave the cave. There was no other way. One by one, we made it out of the cave. With exhilaration and applause, we arrived victorious, achieving our goal. Standing around exposed in the sunlight, we laughed at one another at how grubby we looked covered in mud.

The boarding school students and I loaded onto the bus. We waited until the dorm parents cleaned up and packed the picnic supplies near the cave. I got out of my seat and stood in the aisle. I was talking when suddenly a huge fly flew posthaste directly into my mouth. I remembered that it was a more significant-sized fly than usual. I freaked out and tried to spit it out, but it went down my throat. I returned to my seat, imagining the worst of where the fly was inside me.

The dorm parents loaded the stuff at the back of the bus. We left the site and traveled back. I felt out of sorts in the middle of the trip and had a queasy feeling in my stomach. I got out of my seat and threw up inside the bus aisle. It was nauseating, to say the least. The children withdrew in disgust. The bus stopped. I went outside and threw up several times until I settled down. I told one of the dorm dads that a fly flew into my mouth. When I told him that, he looked at the vomit and pointed to the fly. He and the other dorm dads laughed. The dorm parents cleaned up the mess inside the bus. We continued back home on our trip. I could not wait to shower, wear clean clothes, and go to bed.

It was not very long before I developed a high fever. The nurse fed me soup, crackers, and other comfort foods. The patients' room was all white and spotless. I slept for a couple of days there. I woke up in the middle of the night and had to go to the bathroom. I sat up and looked down. I was afraid. I was sleeping on a hospital bed. It did not have any arm rails. I was so worried that I did not know if I could get down. I started yelling, "Help," for someone to help me to the bathroom. The room was so quiet. I did not hear anyone stirring. I did not know where the nurse was or the school headmaster. I could not hold it, so I soaked the warm urine on the bed. I crawled over the bed and carefully dropped myself onto the floor. I went over to the door, but it was locked. I could not get out. I yelled, "Help," again. Still no reply. My screams were never heard.

Feeling weak, I returned to bed, pulled the sheets down, and dropped them on the floor. Then, I took my wet underwear and nightgown off.

I looked up at the hospital bed and eventually figured out how to climb up there.

After a couple of hours had passed, I roused from my deep sleep and threw up all over myself. This was an awful time, especially when no one was around to help me. I felt so sick that I was not able to move after that. I slept with all of the vomit.

Hours later, I woke up to a bright light. The nurse walked in and headed toward me in haste. She looked at the nauseous potpourri mess and told me I must have had an eventful night.

She washed me up and transferred me onto another clean bed that was more accessible for me to get onto than the one I was on. After that, I felt much better and more comfortable.

It wasn't long after I was on the mend that I started itching my arms while playing in the grand playroom. Concerned, one of my dorm moms yanked my arm up quickly and noticed red spots. She wasted no time and assisted me to the resident nurse's office. I was diagnosed with chicken pox.

I was in the playroom one day. I remember the early spring sun bursting into the grand playroom through the windows. It was glistening so brightly that my eyes squinted. I could also see the dust particles floating in the air from the sunbeams. The place felt warm and peaceful. The thought of my parents and siblings rarely crossed my mind. I felt safe and happy for the first time. It was like a home away from home. Living at the boarding school, surrounded by wonderful people and a healthy environment, began to frame my mind in a new direction.

CHAPTER SIX:

One Step Forward and Two Steps Back

There were barely any children at the boarding school because of the spread of chicken pox. I was one of the few that lingered there. I played with my favorite toys until one of my dorm moms called for me, "Thelma, come here; I have a surprise for you!" I left the toys on the floor, quickly looked over, and approached her. She pointed her finger in one direction; to my shock and dismay, it was my father. He spread his arms open wide and said my name, "Uh-dub-duh," with a smile on his face. He looked on as I screamed in terror and cried. I scrambled quickly behind my dorm mom. I grabbed and clutched onto one of her legs tightly and did not let go. I cried out, "I do not want to go with him. Please, I want to stay here." I cried uncontrollably in desperation for her not to let me go back home with him. My screams were never heard.

My father stood there under the doorway. Quickly, I sensed his wrath as a dark shadow loomed over him. The smile faded, and then he stared at me. My dorm mom gently took my hand, calmed me down, and told me it was time to go home. She had no idea what my father was like behind closed doors.

She smiled at my father as she led me to him. He took my hand, and immediately, everything inside of me froze. I reluctantly yielded my hand to his as I was whisked away from my safe place. My father never talked to me or acknowledged me throughout the trip home. Unfortunately, my imagination got the better of me, and I knew my father well enough to know that the worst was yet to come.

I sat in the front seat of the car next to my father. I yearned to sit in the back seat to get away from him. He was driving a new station wagon with faux wood panel designs on both sides. My father purchased new vehicles every year or two to seek status and acceptance. He could not afford it, but having a new car was a top priority even though we lived from hand to mouth. He knew a car salesman, Bob, who worked at a car dealership. They became good friends; therefore, he could get a good deal on cars. The four-hour trip home with my father made my stomach sick with knots of anxiety. He did not sign a word to me since he picked me up from the boarding school. His countenance was implacable.

My father drove northeast of Indiana to another city named Bristol. We arrived at a trailer park and went on a long, narrow road just before we went toward the dead end. He turned right into a gravel driveway. I looked at my father and the surroundings, wondering where we were at. I had never seen this place.

Our new home was a white trailer with dark brown shutters. My father opened the back of the station wagon to retrieve my suitcase. There were concrete stairs on the side of the trailer. We approached the front door, and my mother and siblings greeted me.

My mother smiled and immediately started signing everything that came to her mind. She never gave me a word in edgewise nor asked about my stay at the boarding school. She told me that my father had retired from his work at a company that made axles for trailers. Because of this, our lives dramatically changed for the worse. My father was entitled to social security benefits. Everyone, including me, received benefits as well. My father was sixty-two years old when I was only seven at that time. Things were headed into another shift from our former way of life. Things seemed materially good before, but now things were different. I longed for a U-turn back to Bloomington.

The trailer home was much different than I was used to with the house we lived in before. The interior panel walls were dark walnut. The carpet was dark brown and shaggy. The living room was simple and had only my father's reclining chair and a couch. On the other side was the tiny black and white television set with two antennas stuck out about a yard long with aluminum foil wrapped around it for better reception.

I realized that I was sent home because I had chicken pox. The boarding school nurse did all she could, but they had to close the entire school down for the remainder of the school year.

The small bumps all over my body now grew worse and more severe. It was so bad that I could not stop itching them. My brother and sister eventually caught the pox, too. We could not play outside; therefore, we watched cartoons and shows on TV. I loved watching my favorite show, *Wonder Woman*. She was my favorite hero. My siblings and I sat on the floor close to the TV with our eyes fixated on it. My mother liked the fact that we never moved away from the TV set. It freed her a lot to do what she wanted around the home.

My mother was a health-conscious person. She did her best according to her knowledge to care for us. Our body temperatures soared, and we were miserably weak. She smacked our hands and told us to stop picking and itching them on our faces and bodies. She bathed us in oatmeal baths and spoon-fed us chicken noodle soup and crackers almost daily for several weeks until the illness subsided.

Father was not around much. He would spend almost all the money on himself to gamble, drink, and bowl every weekend with his friends. He also went to bowling tournaments to win prize money and trophies. He was an outstanding bowler. Once, he took the family and me to an enormous deaf bowling tournament in Chicago. He rarely took us anywhere with him to events such as these. Therefore, getting away somewhere and seeing the world was an exciting time.

My father told my mother to get the mail. As soon as she left, my father demanded I have sex with him and forced me to swear to secrecy not to tell my mother in an intimidating manner. It was the same intimidation tactic he had used on my mother when he often threatened to kill her. Because I could talk better, he felt threatened and had to do everything he could to suppress me. The community mailbox was quite a way down the road. I was told to look out the window for signs of my mother returning while my father violated me.

I could see my mother walking back while pilfering through the mail. I told Father I could see her coming. He quickly left me to go to the bathroom. I pulled up my underwear and pants, feeling like discarded trash and confused. This happened almost every day. I was weary of his demands. I told Mother what he did, but she ignored me. It was a vicious cycle of despair and defeat. Life was not getting better but getting worse. I did not feel like a daughter. I was not treasured or esteemed in my father's eyes. The thought of being a daughter was nothing more than a distant dream. I was shackled in my home as my father viewed me as a convenience for his pleasure.

Whenever I approached Father for anything, he waved his hand at me and shooed me away to leave him alone. Most of the time, he did not like to be bothered while reading the newspaper or watching TV.

Watching my father sit on his reclining chair, I observed that he looked more like a grandfather than a father. I realized he did not look younger than the fathers of kids my age. At that point, I was embarrassed to be seen with an old father in public.

Ever since I left the boarding school, his demands and expectations were on a grander scale. Somehow, he believed I could talk proficiently, but he was wrong.

I was just seven years old, and to make matters worse, he would put me in the spotlight and force me to translate for him. I was dragged to the bank, stores, and even a small claims court to be his translator. When he lost the court case, which involved confusion over a twenty-dollar transaction, he threw a fitful rage at me and blamed me for his loss. I took it personally and believed him. There was nothing that I did that was good enough for my father.

He would shame me in public if something did not go his way. He placed heavy burdens and pressured me to be his crutch. Because I am a CODA, he relied on me for services of what I could do for him rather than to establish a healthy, loving father-and-daughter relationship. He sucked my life out and continued overdrawing when I had nothing left in me to give.

CHAPTER SEVEN:

Living on the Boundary Lines

Toward the end of summer in 1976, we packed up our meager belongings and moved into a two-bedroom house in White Pigeon, Michigan. The house was in a remote area outside of town in the farming country. It was near the boundary line of Indiana. There were cornfields everywhere. On the west side of the road was a town with a small church. Only two neighbors were near us, and several were down the road. The neighbor next to us was an old couple with an older daughter. The one across the street was an old widow who had a German shepherd dog leashed up outside its doghouse twenty-four hours a day and seven days a week.

Our home was constructed, which looked like it was built with concrete blocks and then painted over in a gross-looking light, mint green color. The property had a semi-circle driveway adjacent to one that went straight to the garage from the road. Next to the side of the house stood a large, old, rusted, white propane tank. It looked to be over six feet and looked like an aquatic submarine. The back of the garage had a small tool room with stair steps up to it. It had a secret trap door on the floor used for food storage and as an emergency shelter.

Behind the house was an animal stable and a chicken coop. I stood outside in the backyard, and on the left side were cornfields owned by a commercial company. I gestured to my brother and sister to explore. We took off running into the cornfields.

The cornstalks were tall and lined up in perfect rows. The long green leaves hung over like protruding arms and hands that made clapping sounds from brushing our bodies against them as we ran. After our escapade, we returned to the house exhausted.

While my father and mother were moving things into our new home, I wandered around inside the house. It was small, with two bedrooms and one bath. Since there were five of us, my father had settled into the back corner bedroom all to himself. He was selfish and did not consider my mother or us children first place in his life. He brought dozens of *Playboy* magazines and stacked them inside his closet next to his giant metal container for his discarded coins. The magazines were piled about two feet high. The other bedroom was toward the front corner of the house, where my mother and I shared a queen-sized bed. My brother and sister did not have a bedroom and slept together on a black wool fabric-covered couch in the living room. The floors throughout the house used to have carpet as several nails protruded with carpet yarn remnants stuck on them.

We settled into our routines at the house. My father micromanaged everything in our lives. He forbade any of us to take showers or baths every day. We were only allowed to bathe once weekly on Sunday evenings like clockwork. We were also forced to wear the same clothes every day until Sunday.

After my Sunday bath, my mother rolled every strand of my damp hair onto hair rollers. It had pink sponges and pink plastic clips. Since my hair was clean, my mother only did this once a week. Mother did not like the fact that we bathed once a week. It was a forbidden boundary line that my father laid out. He did not care if we smelled terrible or had oily hair.

The following day, I found some hair rollers that had fallen off on one side of my head during my sleep. My mother took the rest of the rollers off and styled my hair the best she could. It looked odd and dowdy. One side was very curly, and the other was mixed with wavy and straight hair strands. Mother helped with my clothes and gestured in sign language for me to go to the kitchen table.

I spooned brown sugar over my bowl of hot oatmeal with sliced bananas as my mother poured milk into it. Then, finally, she hurried me to eat, hustled me out the door, and told me to stand at the end of the driveway for my bus. It was the first day of school.

I arrived at the elementary school. I followed everyone inside, and I did not know where to go. The principal was a very polite gentleman. He asked my name and showed me my second-grade classroom. He opened the door and introduced me to the teacher, Mrs. Bowman. She showed me my desk, which was next to the door.

I could understand the teacher and talk to everyone since I learned how to speak and read at the boarding school the year prior. Nevertheless, I was mandated to see a tutor daily during school hours so that I would not fall behind.

Having a tutor paid off because I was the fastest reader when we had reading circle time. Even though I no longer needed a tutor to learn how to read, I benefited from it for another couple of years because I was a CODA.

At recess time, I played with a girl named Misty. She was a friendly girl with glasses. Misty became my best friend. I had always looked forward to recess. When it was severely cold outside, we played inside the gym.

I remember the 1976 blizzard. It was so bad that it covered up our windows and doors with over five feet of snow. Father had to shovel the snow by hand. The school was canceled.

During P.E., the gym teacher took his clipboard and recorded each student to see who could shoot the most baskets to qualify for the Hoop Shoot Contest. Shockingly, I was one of the top scorers two years in a row. My hand and eye coordination were excellent because my sign language communication skills mainly relied on my eyes, not my ears. School activities gave me a boost of confidence when I had none. It helped fill the gaps that my father never filled.

HIGH SCORERS — Winners of the White Pigeon Elementary School Hoop Shoot include (front, from left) Mike Wood, 12-13 age group and Tim Baechler, 10-11 group. Back: Diane Nottoli, 12-13; Thelma Therrien, 10-11; Tresa Sweltzer, 8-9; and Mark McLane, 8-9. Baechler and Wood were high shooters, with 16 out of 25 attempts. The contest, sponsored by the Three Rivers Elks Lodge, was the first step to district, state and national contests, with all expenses paid by the Elks organization. The awards to the White Pigeon youngsters were presented by Vernon Wickman, chairman of the Elks Hoop Shoot committee. The next contest will be Dec. 9 in Three Rivers Junior High School and will pit about 25 school champions against each other, including entrants from Constantine, Centreville, Mendon, Nottawa, Schoolcraft, Three Rivers, Union and White Pigeon.

Winners of the 1996 White Pigeon Elementary School Hoop Shoot; I am second from the left, standing in the back.

*I am pictured on the left along with other top scorers
in the 1977 Hoop Shoot Contest.*

At gym time, the girls and I were engrossed in gymnastics. We were determined to teach ourselves cartwheels and back walk-overs. The girls and I raced to the gym to get on the exercise mat. Otherwise, we had to stand in line to wait our turn. We practiced for many weeks until we mastered them and finally did it. Those school years were fun and fulfilling, except when I was at home.

CHAPTER EIGHT:

Steal, Kill, and Destroy

My family and I went to the local bank. I had to go and assist my father and mother in interpreting for them. It was intimidating to be the translator for both my parents. Their dependence on me was unhealthy and too much for me to bear. They expected me to be there for them, but there was never any reciprocation. I was their full-time assistant. Back then, there was no sign language interpreter nearby that my father and mother could call on for assistance.

We were next in line when my mother came across savings booklets on a display case, which was an introduction to learning how to save. She picked up the booklet that had unique slots to fit quarters. She loved the idea, and I translated for her, requesting three booklets for each of us children.

She put a quarter in each booklet for us. I was thrilled to have my very own savings booklet. She said we would bring it back to the bank to deposit into a savings account when it was filled.

She was notorious for saving every coin. After many months, our booklets were all filled with quarters. Mother opened the savings accounts. She requested more booklets to save more quarters. My father caught wind of it and withdrew all our money to buy beer and chewing tobacco. When my mother told me about it, I was heartbroken that he had stolen all our money to use on himself. Mother did not give up; she kept saving quarters, but this time, she did not deposit them in the bank. She hid them. But again, Father found her stash and stole it. It was frustrating, to be sure.

No matter how hard we tried to move forward or make baby steps, our efforts were destroyed, and we had to start over again. No matter how little or big it was, it was stolen. This was how we lived in every single area of our lives. My father was a thief and tore down everything. Having everything stolen from me became the norm. It was a way of life. My mother never spoke up and faced defeat at every turn. Learning to accept defeat opened another door for the enemy to lay a firm stronghold by claiming everything in our lives to steal, kill, and destroy.

I went to the bathroom and grabbed my toothbrush that had worn curled bristles and some leftover mint green toothpaste lodged deep inside it. As I brushed my teeth, I looked at my left front tooth, which protruded and overlapped permanently over the right one. Mother promised me that I would get braces one day. She meant well, but we lived in poverty. I became self-conscious about it and barely smiled. If I had to talk, I ensured no one saw my teeth.

After I left the bathroom, my father approached me. He looked around, acting like he did not want to be caught in some scheme. It was obvious to me, and I was uncomfortable about what evil he was plotting next to conceive. I turned around quickly to avoid him and went to my bedroom. "Uh-dub-duh," vociferated Father. I stopped and glanced back at him with vexation. He gave me orders that he wanted me to go to his bedroom when everyone was asleep. He told me he would sound out my name for me to go directly to his bedroom. He also instructed me to quietly leave my bed without waking my mother.

As a daughter, I yearned deep down in my heart, clamoring for a daddy. I was a sex slave and a prisoner in my home with invisible chains that had snatched my soul into the abyss of despair. This man completely controlled the blank slate of my childhood innocence. He was the doorkeeper of my soul. My mind, will, and emotions were controlled by him. I was not allowed to think, say, or feel. His briberies and undercurrent threats created room in my mind to remain silent, although he did not know that I told my mother. As a result, my mind had constant turmoil of fear and unrest.

I asked my father why my mother could not sleep with him and even told him that he was supposed to sleep with her because they were married. I spoke in a childlike directness and frankly told him the truth, knowing that fathers and daughters do not have sex. He argued that sex with my mother was stale. He signed to me perverse details about how he was attracted to my body parts. He had no shame. It wasn't easy to process why he did what he did to me and why he said what he said. I could not wrap my head around this unnatural reply and felt uncomfortable. He then continued and said that he and I would get married. Speechless, I looked at my father in disgust and suddenly had a nauseous feeling in my stomach. I did not want to marry my aged father. I saw him in a different light and knew I was living with a monster. I looked down and looked away and wanted to hide. I was terribly afraid to do anything except comply with his demands. Coldly, he then shooed me away. I walked into my bedroom with a stabbing pit in my stomach. I felt like a soulless nobody.

I went to bed with my mother. She was already tucked in bed. I pressed the back of my body against her warm back. She reached out her hand behind her and searched for my hand. I put my hand in hers. She squeezed my hand with affection and then released it slowly as I knew she was falling asleep.

I nestled securely next to her and under the warm blankets as if that would protect me. I hoped against all hope that Father would fall asleep. I began psyching myself up and hoped it would not happen that night. I then tried to go to sleep.

Shortly after a while, I woke to my father's guttural voice, "Uh-dub-duh." He repeated it a couple more times. I reluctantly slinked down from the bed and tiptoed in the dark. I was very sleepy. I passed the living room, where my brother and sister slept together on the couch. On the right was the bathroom. I walked past it. It got darker as I groped my hand around in the darkness, finding my way toward the end of the hallway. Edging near the end with trepidation, my father gestured with his hand for me to come in. It felt like claws from a demon that reached out from hell and snatched me in. He closed the door and stripped my pajamas off. He signed to me and told me to touch his privates. I resisted his demand. He then forced my hand, and as soon as I felt something, I quickly pulled away, horrified. Without effort, he viciously picked me up with the massive strength of his hand and threw me on the bed. With all my power, I bounced out of his bed crying and desperately ran toward the door. He grabbed his black leather belt and swatted me several times to control me. He picked me up, forcefully laid me on the bed, and raped me. My screams were never heard.

I was only seven years old, and the sexual abuse continued several times a week for over five years until I started my period at twelve. The beltings and lashings continued until I caved into his demands. I had red striped lines and bruises on my thighs, hips, butt, and back. *Why won't my mother believe me?* I thought to myself.

I became compliant, allowing everyone to run over me like a doormat. I became a person who was a people pleaser and adaptable to be like others. I did not know who I was. I had no identity. My father controlled my life. He forced me to submit to him. He put me in a position where I had no choice except to comply with his demands. I did not want him or other people to be angry at me. I was looking for love and acceptance everywhere. I sought approval at school and even did homework for a popular girl in my fourth-grade class while she played outside at recess time.

———

During those five years of torment in White Pigeon, I distinctly remember that on one of those episodes, I heard my father calling my name, "Uh-dub-duh."

This time, I did not get out of bed.

Chapter Eight: Steal, Kill, and Destroy   103

He raised the tone of his voice louder, "Uh-dub-duh." I panicked and lay frozen in a fetal position on my bed, covered with a blanket.

Then again, he did it in a tone full of rage, "Uh-dub-duh!" It sounded like a demon.

His anger sent chills through my body.

Breathing nervously, I felt my body shake as I peeked out from under the blanket, looking at where the bedroom door was at. I heard his voice make a long, undercurrent, angry, mumbling sound in rage and frustration. He finally stopped calling me.

I wanted my mother to protect me, but my job was to protect her. I wanted her to sleep next to the bedroom door instead of me. The roles were reversed. I was responsible for caring for my mother's emotional and physical needs. I felt like I was her emotional support animal. In my father's eyes, I replaced my mother as my father's pretend wife.

I developed panic attacks and could barely breathe every night. Even after those episodes with my father, I could not sleep well because the darkness scared me, and I was in so much pain. For many years, I barely ever had a peaceful sleep. Everyone was asleep except me. Hearing my father snore every night was a good sign that I could go to bed peacefully.

I had imagined he would come into the bedroom and hurt me, but he never dared to do it with my mother present. I never knew if my mother had ever told my father what I shared with her about the sexual abuse throughout my childhood. My mother knew that my father was sexually abusing me, but she chose to deny the truth and accused me of imagining those stories. I could see the fear in her eyes. I was trapped between a father who abused me and a mother who ignored me.

The next day, my father was in a bad mood. He approached me with a look of disapproval and wildly signed at me in anger as to why I did not go to his bedroom that night. I lied to him and said that I must have fallen asleep. He blew up in a towering rage, fuming with guttural sounds, and called me a liar. I stood there trembling quietly, feeling powerless and worried about what he would do next. He shamed me for being a bad girl and signed specific words in sign language that I was a piece of scrap and a reject. I retreated to my bedroom, opened the wooden bi-fold closet doors, crawled over the boxes and a laundry basket filled with clothes and toys, closed the doors, and hid in the dark. As my eyes adjusted to the darkness inside the closet, I looked over and saw my Barbie doll. I grabbed it, held it close for comfort, and cried in paralyzing hopelessness.

I could hear my father watching the news on TV. A well-known sign language interpreter named Norma was prominent in the deaf community and translated local TV news in the area. I heard Father get up from his reclining chair, and to my chagrin, he farted super loudly.

I waited until the right moment to tell my mother what had happened. When I heard my father leave, I told my mother that Father was hurting me sexually. I lifted my shirt and pulled down my pants to show her my lash marks and bruises. She rapidly moved her head from left to right, which meant "no." Her face was pinched, her hands were flailing at me in sign language, and she told me it was untrue. She knew that Father was raping me, but she feared getting killed. I also brought it up during my Sunday baths to show her the bruises and lashings on my body, but she continually refused to acknowledge the truth by simply ignoring me.

As a girl, I had always sensed that my mother was incapable of caring for me because she was emotionally abused by my father, too. She had gotten worse mentally as the years went on. I had told my mother many times, but she ignored me and told me to think happy thoughts. It was futile.

There were many times that Mother locked Ted, Dottie, and me outside the house. We did not know why she did that. It was frustrating. My siblings and I frequently climbed a particular tree that stood next to the house. We climbed the tree as high as we could go. We knew every branch on that tree. I had a favorite spot where I felt safe. I just sat and hid there until Mother finally let us into the house.

Mother talked about anything that came to her mind and repeated it. I never understood why she did that. I can't recall her taking the time to listen to me and share anything from my heart. My mother exasperated me because she talked too much and did not know when to stop. I sat and looked at her patiently as she signed anything that came to her mind. I was my mother's crutch. She stopped me from sharing my feelings and ignored me when I would interject and say something. I sat patiently until she was distracted by something else.

I truly believed that no one cared about what I had to say. My mind was in a fog and was stunted emotionally and mentally from the traumas, neglect, and abuse. I was like a fawn standing in the middle of the road, staring at the bright headlights of an approaching car driving at full speed, ready to run me over. I was not able to process, think, or make decisions. Life hit me in every direction. I did not know how to think because I was not allowed to think. It was so dysfunctional that it felt like I was in a coma.

I was not able to wake up from the hellish nightmare. My mind transcended into a comatose state from the constant abuse. To escape, I developed bad habits. Overeating food was one of the ways that helped me get through temporarily. I also plucked all my eyebrows and eyelashes until almost nothing was left. I also took nail clippers and cut my hair with them. I tore my fingernails and chewed the skin off the inside of my mouth. I was a nervous wreck. I often went to my bedroom in the farthest corner and sat on the floor near my mother's bedside to be alone.

I played my records on the record player. Eventually, I did get sick and tired of hearing these, but they were the only records I had ever owned since I was five. As I listened to the records, it transported me to a faraway place that felt safe. It was not reality, but it helped me escape hell as a child.

My favorite was *Sleeping Beauty*. I had dreamed that someday someone would wake me up from the curse and coma that rendered my life helpless.

While I listened to the record player, I played with my dolls. I had a gift of creativity and made my dollhouse furniture from used matchboxes and toilet paper tubes and sewed doll clothes from scraps of fabric material. I created paper inventions and designed a dream home and family I had always wanted through my dolls.

There were also only two books on the shelf that we owned. One was a paperback book of *The Wizard of Oz* that I had read dozens of times. The second was a hardcover book with shiny embossed print with a fancy font on the front cover. It was a children's Bible. I recalled the visitor at the front door representing a religious entity selling these books mainly for children. My mother perused the pages of the copy of the book and offered to buy it. I did not know how much it cost then, but she got a jar of coins and poured it on the table. She counted the menagerie of coins into a pile until it equaled one dollar. She told me to help her. We repeated the process until we had enough money for the book. The visitor stared at us as we counted the coins. My mother was excited to have enough money to pay for the children's Bible. It was the only Bible that we owned in our home. It was not actually a Bible per se, but it was close. I was intrigued by the colorful pictures and stories. It was wonderful, except for one part about the angels of God from heaven marrying daughters of men on earth. I had always struggled with that story. It reminded me of my father when he told me he wanted to marry me.

The one story that intrigued me the most was the story about Joseph. The lesson I learned from him was that he stayed faithful to his God and did his best despite everything he went through.

Even though the person who sold us the children's Bible was from a different religious entity, it was not an accident.

God used that person so that I could have a Bible. It got me through as I learned about God. He used it to help my faith. So, even though we could not afford it, it was a huge surprise for me to see my mother determined to get the book, especially from her secret coin stash.

CHAPTER NINE:

Taking Hysteria Out of Hysterectomy

My mother was a clean freak and often had all the windows open around the house for fresh air. The wind blew the cotton curtains. It swirled around like a dance and tossed back and forth as if an invisible, sleeping giant wind exhaled the curtains out and inhaled, sucking them back against the screen window.

Mother melodramatically inhaled a deep breath as she signed to me how the fresh air purges away stink and filth. She cleaned the house with a solid pine-scented cleaner that she swore killed every germ.

Suddenly, a hot flash came all over her. She acted like she was on fire. She looked around, grabbed one of my father's newspapers, and fanned her face to cool herself down. I could see that her face and neck had turned red. It was like watching the red indicator of an oral thermometer rising. We had one in our medicine cabinet that contained mercury liquid inside a stick-shaped glass container. It would rise and then stop to show the exact body temperature. She told me she had made an appointment to see a doctor within the next couple of weeks.

Out of nowhere, I heard music blaring from a distance. I went outside to find out who the passersby were. The music got louder as it got closer and closer. I gawked outside expecting an ice cream truck, but it was a late 1970s bright turquoise Volkswagen van. It slowed down and entered our black tarred semi-circle driveway in front of our house. The decibel of the music was ear-piercing. But whatever it was, it was better than the ice cream truck's music. The bombinations from the bass could be felt from several feet away.

I stood staring outside and listened to the booming van jams. It was as if the driver brought the entire disco dance floor to our home. The man jumped out of the van, took his cigarette out of his mouth, and placed it between his two stubby fingers as he waved his hand and gleefully greeted me in a high-pitched slow-motion tone, "Heyyyyyyy!" I could tell he was deaf by how he said it. His voice sounded so much like the cartoon character Popeye, the Sailor Man. The man smiled a toothless smile that showed only his gums. He wore hearing aids in both ears. My brother and sister had the same kind of hearing aids as his. The hearing aids had wires connecting the earpieces to a transistor worn over the chest with shoulder straps.

I remembered this man from when I was little and recalled meeting him during the Christmas season at the mall where he worked as a janitor. He was a short, bald man with a nice tan and bloodshot eyes from drinking too much beer. On the van's passenger side, his wife stepped out and gently blew cigarette smoke from her bright, red-painted lips. The smoke billowed and disappeared into thin air. She was gorgeous with long, straight blonde hair and thick black clumpy eyelashes. She was dressed in bell-bottom pants and a pretty shirt. She was a foot taller than her husband. She was hard of hearing but could speak very well as she greeted me with a pleasant smile. I ran inside the house to find my father and mother and told them we had company.

My family came out, and at once, everyone was signing small talk and laughing together. The music was still blaring from the van as Father asked me in front of everyone if I remembered Ezra. I nodded my head with a yes. Ezra's wife's name was Delilah.

The van doors were wide open. It beckoned me to go inside. I helped myself as I crawled onto the passenger seat and basked in the music. It felt so good to listen to it loudly. The sensation I got was like a waterfall sweeping over me. Ezra walked around and sat in the driver's seat. He placed his cigarette on one side of his mouth and showed me his eight-track music cassette tapes of different popular groups. I noticed that next to the music tapes were Ezra's dentures. He turned the music up higher. I looked at him with curiosity at how free and happy he looked. It was something I wanted that I did not have with my family. He then ejected the eight-track tape and showed me how to insert it carefully into the eight-track player. Next, Ezra grooved and danced to "Funkytown" by Lipps Inc. in the van. He jammed his cigarette into the tray, laughed, and flailed his arms to the beat of the music. I giggled as I watched him make his dance moves. I was captivated by him as he was engaging and entertaining. I liked him a lot. "Funkytown" hit home with me, and I played it repeatedly because I eventually knew I would not hear music for a long time after he and Delilah left. He instantly became my favorite deaf person. Before Ezra and Delilah left, he invited all of us to go to the public beach and hang out together that coming weekend.

For the next few years, going to the beach with Ezra and Delilah was something I always looked forward to. I was thankful and glad that Ezra initiated efforts to get my family together with them. Unfortunately, my father and Ezra got stoned drunk every time we went.

My brother, sister, and I swam most of the day in the water. Ezra would pick us up individually, throw us, and dunk us in the lake. It was so much fun. My father never played with us children. He was flirting with Delilah while my mother sat under the cool shade of a tree to avoid sunburn.

Photo taken at the beach with my mother sitting on the lounge chair. My brother and sister are standing behind us.

I approached Ezra and told him that something was stuck on my leg. He laughed and said it was a leech. My father approached with a cold beer in his hand. Ezra thought he had a great idea and grabbed my father's beer and stuck it onto the leech. I freaked out. Both men were tipsy and were laughing at the scenario. I begged in desperation, asking them to please help remove it. Ezra kept putting the beer can on it, thinking it would help remove it. Finally, my father found a stick and pried it off. It seemed forever to remove it because it felt like a weird thing with suction cups.

By sunset, our energy was expended. We were waterlogged and sunburnt. We packed our coolers, lawn chairs, and beach towels into the cars and headed our separate ways.

Mother was terrified of riding in the front passenger side while father drove the car, especially while he was under the influence of alcohol. She constantly signed and gestured to him to stay in his lane because he was swerving on the road. It was a miracle that we made it home alive. When we got home, my father looked like he was doubled over in pain and ran fast to the bathroom and vomited. It was one of those moments when I wished he would always stay drunk so that he would not hurt me and the family.

My mother went to her doctor's appointment to get tests done. Unfortunately, the diagnosis results came back positive. It indicated that she had tumors in her ovaries and was scheduled immediately for a hysterectomy.

As the time came for her to have surgery, my siblings and I stayed at Aunt Alice and Uncle Chet's house. My aunt Alice, my mother's sister, had no deaf children. However, she had two children that were CODAs like me. My cousins were Jane, who was about the same age as me, and Sean, who was seven years older. He had moved out of their house recently to live with Grandpa Gerry and Grandma Pearl.

Grandpa gave up his bedroom for Sean and slept in a separate bed in the same room with Grandma. My uncle John was deaf and had a bedroom to himself. He never married nor had any children. He lived as a peace-loving man and worked a steady job to help support Grandpa and Grandma. He lived in the same house most of his life.

Jane was a well-adjusted daughter. She had everything going for her. She was loved and nurtured by Uncle Chet and Aunt Alice. Of course, my mother and Aunt Alice were quite different in personalities. Although Aunt Alice was deaf, she was a stable, sane person with common sense.

Uncle Chet was not deaf. He talked to me often and treated me with dignity and respect as if I was one of his daughters. I felt safe in their home and even imagined them adopting me.

In another room in their home was Uncle Chet's elderly mother, who lay on a hospital bed. She was so aged that he and Aunt Alice cared for her until her death. Uncle Chet shared with me that she was part Indian. Everything made sense to me because I had often wondered why his skin was so deeply tanned. I watched Aunt Alice gently change, wash, and towel dry her frail body. She then clothed and bundled her with a bed sheet and blanket to keep her warm. Uncle Chet's mother was not coherent and needed to be looked after round-the-clock.

Later, Aunt Alice drove Jane, my siblings, and me in her gold Impala to Grandpa and Grandma's house. My cousin Sean was there watching Bruce Lee and *The Incredible Hulk* shows. He was a huge fan. So, he invited us to his bedroom to watch TV together. Since Sean was the oldest cousin and was in high school then, we all respected him.

After the shows, my brother, sister, and I jumped on Sean's bed while he showed us karate moves and wrestled with us. He loved wrestling with my brother Ted and would lift him to the ceiling and bump his head on it. Sean was a fun person to hang out with. There was never a dull moment with him.

My father and mother came to pick us up after her surgery. She was still recovering, so she stayed in the car. We scrambled to get our belongings and headed out to the car. We did not wear seat belts. My brother, sister, and I sat at the back of the blue and white SUV my father had recently purchased. I asked my father if I could turn on the radio in the car. I would sit next to the window and exhale vapors from my breath onto the window to create condensation. I pressed the side of my palm to make a pretend baby foot and pressed my fingers to make toes. My brother and sister joined in. We condensed the windows with our breaths. We played tic-tac-toe. After every game, we wiped the car windows with our hands. Imagination was all that we could afford as children.

I took the yarn out of my pocket that was already tied into a knot. I wove it around my fingers to play cat's cradle with my sister. There were a lot of steps and sequences to get it right. I had practiced long enough until I was proficient at it. It was a popular yarn trick I learned from my friends at school.

The car ride home from Grandpa and Grandma's house was about thirty minutes. We arrived home. Mother walked slowly into the house. She asked me to put a blanket and pillow on the couch for her to lie down on. I remember my mother was very fragile and frail. I did everything she asked me to do to make her feel comfortable.

Father sat on his reclining chair, read the newspaper, and watched TV. He complained about having nothing to eat since my mother was unable to cook. So, we got by eating Wheaties cereal. We also made peanut butter and jelly sandwiches by ourselves. I served it to my mother, too.

Mother could not sleep in the bedroom because it was too high for her to crawl up. The couch was the only option.

After a couple of days, my mother was getting worse. She developed a severe fever while she was recovering from her hysterectomy. My father was inconvenienced by not having her around to do all the work for him. It made him increasingly angry that he complained about it to her. She lay on the couch helpless, and tears swelled in her eyes. My father was in hysteria. In sign language, he signed curse words in anger while his veins protruded from the sides of his temples. His face was red, and his eyes were wildly out of control. His voice uttered in rage that caused me to be afraid for her. He told her that he wished she were dead. He went on and on about how tired he was of her always being sick and not feeling well. I yielded carefully toward Mother, placed my hand on her hair, and stroked it. I sat on the floor next to Mother to guard her while Father continued his frenzy. I did not want Mother to look at him, nor did I. My mother broke down in tears in front of my father, and her cries worsened right after he walked away.

Mother's crying spell caused her breathing to go out of control. It was a cry from a broken heart. Mother gave a loud shrill. I laid my head on her shoulder and cried out with her.

I became more convinced that our lives were hopeless. Our screams were never heard.

I was terrified for her life because my father had repeatedly confessed that he had killed men in Chicago. He had no remorse when he shared that information with me. I did not want her to die because if she did, I was afraid my father would make me marry him.

CHAPTER TEN:

Survival Mode

It was that time of the month when money and food supplies became scarce. I opened the refrigerator, and there was nothing to eat. The only thing I saw was a few condiments. The light inside the fridge was bright and showed leftover food crumbs, exposing them on the cold shelves. With the empty refrigerator running, it made no sense to leave it on. I closed the door and then scoured the cupboard shelves. There was rice, oats, and a box with individually wrapped stacks of saltine crackers. I took one of the stacks, went to the living room, lay on the couch with the blanket over my head, and relished each salty bite of the crackers.

Like a whirlwind, the blanket swirled in the air as Father pulled it off me. I was caught in the middle of enjoying my snack. Father berated me for eating the crackers and jerked them from my hands. He quickly went to the bedroom and came out with his black leather belt. My heart dropped, and I fled outside the house and ran as fast as possible, but running away from him was impossible. He chased after me with the belt in hand. When he finally caught up to me, he seized me by grabbing my hair. I stopped with my head yanked back. He pushed me down on the ground and whipped my back, butt, and legs. Indeed, I had hoped the neighbors would come out to help me, but my screams were never heard.

I lay outside with my face down and cried for a long time. My snot was hanging out. My hands shook as I grabbed onto the tall grass blades. I felt I had no more breath left in me. As I lay face down on the earth, I wanted to dig a hole, bury myself, and never come out.

My family lived from hand to mouth. Father quickly spent the money that came in. When barely any food was left, my father and mother made me walk to the neighbor's house and beg for money. I did not particularly want to beg, but we were hungry. I was so embarrassed as I knocked on the door. I brought a handwritten message from my mother that asked them if we could borrow five dollars, or sometimes it was ten dollars to buy food to tie us over until the social security checks came. But, of course, my father always paid them back.

Back then, a loaf of bread was thirty-five cents, and milk cost around $1.70 a gallon. It was enough money to get essentials to feed everyone. Unfortunately, our initial food supply only lasted almost the first three weeks of every month, and then we went hungry. Therefore, we borrowed money from the neighbors. It seemed when I went to beg that the neighbors always had expected me to come at the fourth week toward the end of each month. It was a vicious monthly cycle of hunger and survival.

Just a few days before the social security checks would arrive in the mail, my father and mother talked about how excited they were to get them. That was the only topic of conversation and the only time they got along with each other. My father was in a great mood whenever the social security checks came. It was predictable like clockwork. We would go directly to the bank first to cash the checks. Then, without delay, we went to the grocery store. Grocery shopping was a big deal for my family.

We loaded the grocery cart until there was no more room to fill it. My father sometimes browsed at magazines while my mother did all the shopping. I wandered around the store with my brother and sister.

One time, I spotted my father at an aisle and approached him when suddenly, he let out a foul, repulsive fart. It was so loud that it could be heard several aisles down. My father did not notice his surroundings while looking at a grocery item. It was as if he did not know he had done it. My mouth gaped at what happened, and then my eyes darted at a lady near my father in the same aisle who glared at him in disgust and shock. She covered her nose and steered her cart quickly away from him in one direction, and I walked away from him in the other. I pretended I did not know him as I scurried to find my mother to tell her what happened.

After the shopping trip, we unloaded the groceries into the kitchen. My brother, sister, and I wanted to eat very desperately. My mother gathered us at the kitchen table. We hungrily watched her mix and stir a smooth, creamy concoction of peanut butter and pancake syrup into a bowl. It was a poor man's snack version. It was served with saltine crackers. It was my favorite childhood treat, as I looked forward to it every month after our grocery sprees. We attacked it like ravenous beasts as we scooped the crackers into the dip and devoured it until it vanished.

My father discovered a way to earn money by picking up aluminum scraps for quick and easy cash. It became an obsession. He went to various local garbage dumps and landfills. To survive financially, we often went together as a family to these places. The landfills were unsafe to walk on, and they reeked terribly. I once reclaimed a forty-five-vinyl record of the song "Uncle Albert/Admiral Halsey" by Paul and Linda McCartney. I gently blew on the record to remove the dust and then wiped it off with the end tails of my shirt. The comical and whimsical song spoke directly to me. I was just a little girl, but listening to the song helped release my bottled tears. It was as if someone was talking to me directly, saying, "I'm sorry that you're going through hell, so here's a tune to cheer you up."

There was an underlying desperation of needing to be heard as a CODA, but it felt like an invisible cage over my mind and a muzzle over my mouth. As the abuse from my father continued and worsened over the years, I did not know how to speak, feel, or exactly word my feelings. I was never permitted to express them. I was in a paralyzed state of mind. The different names and labels of abuse and trauma I faced conglomerated into a ball of knotted confusion and fused in my entire psyche. It was as if I were not human at all. Father dehumanized me. I was the only one who could recognize those feelings. I could feel it but did not know how to cure it. No one could ever see what I was going through. After all, who could see inside my brain?

My communication with hearing people was mostly foreign to me. I would stare at them with no expression on my face because I had limited experience interacting with them verbally. My mind gathered the verbiage data of what they were trying to communicate to me through their vocal inflections, mood, and tone. However, I was able to relate well what they were saying by reading their facial and body expressions. Eventually, I could understand mostly what they were trying to say or even what they were thinking. I even could pick up the scent and detect the slightest hints of good or bad, yet I could not label each feeling into words.

There was a weak side of me that was very gullible. I was very hopeful and tried to see the good in every person. Therefore, I fell prey whenever my father pretended to be a nice guy and played with my mind to believe what he promised to do, but it was a sham. I realized later in life that my father did not ever want a relationship or restoration. He was a proud, arrogant, and self-serving person.

If people were so quick to buy medicine for a cough or a cold or even to get help for an injured person physically, what aid was there at the store to help those abused emotionally? I remembered seeing a box of Band-Aids on the bathroom shelf and wished there was an emotional Band-Aid for my broken heart, but there was nothing for it. I did not have the capacity or understanding of how to heal it or make those feelings disappear. All the abuse, the names, and the labels controlled my life. Looking back, I felt shamed, imprisoned, afraid, used, lost, hopeless, rejected, stupid, isolated, dehumanized, worthless, ugly, and like I did not belong. *Is there a place or somebody that can help?* I thought.

One summer, my father wanted me to go with him to the local garbage site to find aluminum. I had looked forward to it since we had been doing it with the family. He had me sit next to him in the front seat while driving and then told me to take the steering wheel. Driving the car with my father on the country road was thrilling. Other sides of my father were fun, but he would use the fun side to manipulate and take advantage of me.

We stopped the van at the garbage site. He opened the van's side door and then pulled his pants down. My trust in him quickly vanished. I looked around the landscape, which was stockpiled with garbage everywhere. The stench was nauseating. I had believed that we were going on a treasure hunt for aluminum. He demanded and forced that I lay down inside the van and let him know if I heard any noise or a car approaching. I told him that I wanted to go home. He did not respond to my plea and exerted his weight against my will. I was weightless and in so much pain from the impact of the rape because he was six feet three inches tall and over 250 pounds. His eyes and face intensified a mood of fierceness and violence. I was in dread of him taking my life.

My father drove and headed home as I sat in the front passenger seat and leaned my shoulder and head against the window. Feeling depressed, I studied the details of every home and road sign we passed. I felt displaced that my father did not want to spend time with me doing fun things such as going out for ice cream or playing a board game together. It was all about him, regardless of my feelings and needs. He lied and manipulated me into believing we were going on an excursion, turning it into a well-laid trap. No matter how much I hoped for a normal, healthy father-and-daughter relationship, it was dashed every time, but I kept hoping.

I imagined opening the car door and falling out to kill myself. It would have been better to die than to endure living with father. Thoughts of suicide had been prevalent in my mind because I had seen my father talk about death and killing almost every day. He had succeeded in mastering control and forming my identity. Father often told me that I was stupid, good for nothing, and a piece of scrap. Those words formed my identity. I felt used and was never appreciated as a human being. Those thoughts quickly vanished when my eyes were transfixed at a church up ahead of the road. I stared at the small building. My head turned slowly sideways as we passed it at fifty-five miles per hour on the country road. I kept staring at it and wondered what it would be like to attend there and hear stories about Jesus. Deep down, something inside me was burning and yearning for more of this Jesus. *Where is He?* I thought. Seeing that church stirred up an image of myself attending there. I had a longing in my heart to follow Jesus, but I was living in hell with the devil.

In the middle of a blazing hot summer, my mother was busy working on an oil painting on canvas for a client. She had sold quite a few in the past. It was a beautiful ocean scape scene that depicted a storm. The details and colors of grays and deep blues perfectly matched the feeling of the tumultuous storm.

It had a ship in the distance that struggled against the gusts of the gale-force winds. Her paint strokes of the waves of water with sea foam touched on the edges were graphic and lifelike. Mother had a gift for art. It ran on the side of her family. It helped her escape from the emotional abuse from my father even though her mental state was worsened by the constant death threats he made.

He rushed her to hurry with the artwork. My mother was crushed under pressure even though she wanted to ensure the painting suited the client's tastes. Eventually, when the oil painting was finished, she sold it for five hundred dollars. My father took all the money and went to Chicago for the weekend. My mother crumbled into pieces mentally and emotionally.

Since then, she had no desire to paint again.

I was in sixth grade and at an awkward stage of my life. I felt like an outsider as my friends and other students in the school were involved in band, sports, and other fun hobbies. The music teacher shared information about various musical instruments they offered through a company to rent or buy from. He also said there was a sign-up sheet if we wanted to join the school band. I signed up and brought home an order form to purchase a musical instrument. I begged my father and mother that I wanted to play the clarinet, but they said no. Because they could not hear, I was not permitted. I was frustrated as a CODA with all of the limitations of being unable to participate like other hearing children.

Misty invited me to join Girl Scouts. My father's response was a firm, emphatic "no." Misty's mother was the troop leader in the area, and she reached out and visited my father to share information with him that they did crafts, camping, and other fun activities. After being persuaded, my father let me join. My parents could not afford a uniform, but regardless, it was so much fun to be with Misty and to get away from home.

I am pictured on the left, along with my friends from Girl Scouts, before our march in a parade.

At twelve, I was extremely uncultured, teeter-tottering between the deaf and English-speaking cultures. I was very insecure and copied every move and every word those girls did at school. I was such a nervous wreck around people that I wanted to please everyone to feel I belonged. A few students made fun of me for wearing the same clothes every day at school and teased my first name. This awakened me to realize they were right. I had not thought of that before because I was drilled by my father to wear soiled pants from yesterday's recess to school the following day and every day until Sunday.

Although my father forbade us to change our clothes and bathe every day, I no longer wanted to be teased. I dug around in my closet to find other clothes I could wear each day of the week. There were a few, and I did my best to make it work. My mother did not like me disrupting the order of the home because she would have to bear the brunt of my father. I asked my mother why I could not shower every day because my scalp was already oily by the end of the week. I became dirtier and smellier, which was perhaps why no one wanted to be near me at school. My mother acknowledged it and did what she could to wash my hair often when my father was not around. When my father drove away to go somewhere, she told me to hurry to the bathroom. She washed my hair in the sink and sent me outside to let it air dry because we never owned or could afford a hairdryer. She helped towel dry it to further the speeding process before Father returned home. It felt so good to be clean.

CHAPTER ELEVEN:

Earth, Wind, and Fire

I remember one vivid moment in the summer of 1980. I was twelve years old at the time. I stepped out of my bedroom and followed my mother into the living room as she took my underwear with blood stains to show my father. She waved it before his face to get his attention and informed him that my period had started. She taunted him and danced around in a circle as if she had triumphed in victory. I was so embarrassed by her indiscreet display. He sat on his reclining chair, stared at her with a cold, steely look, and did not reply.

My stomach hurt, and I was bleeding so much that I thought I was dying. No one explained to me about menstruation. I was in so much pain when it started. Finally, my mother hurriedly told my father to make an emergency trip to the store to get feminine sanitary pads. After he returned, my mother was in disbelief that my father purchased a box of baby diapers. Father did it to spite her, yet simultaneously, he humiliated me. He told my mother he was not returning to the store and told her to use them. I had no idea what was happening and why I had to wear diapers.

Mother pointed her finger, directing me to march straight to the bedroom. She told me to lie down on the bed. As a pre-teen, I was so embarrassed as I lay naked before her. She put the diaper under my bottom, folded up the front, adjusted the sides so tightly on my waist, and adhered it with the diaper closures. I was terribly skinny at my age; therefore, I could fit into it. The box had a picture of a baby wearing diapers. I did not like the fact that I was forced to wear them. Everything in my mind knew this was not normal, but the abnormal became my normal way of life.

Starting my period had been a concern for my mother because she did not want me to be pregnant by my father.

It was very cloudy and windy, with gentle light showers outside that day. My mother ran to me with a face that displayed pure terror. She frantically gestured to me in sign language to leave the house immediately. I obeyed her at once, even though I had no idea what was happening. Her fear spilled over to me. Somehow, something had transpired between my father and mother outside in the backyard.

I did not know what happened, but it was so extremely grave that I had never seen her act this way. I instantly knew we were on the fringes of danger or even death. My heart was beating fast, and my breathing was a struggle. My hands were sweating and shaking, knowing my father, all too well, had told my mother that he would do what he had constantly threatened to do for many years. Father had always threatened to kill her and all of us together.

Whatever it was, it caused a flight response instead of a fight response. Mother knew we had to get to safety as soon as possible. So, we fled from the house and ran toward the road on U.S. 12. My brother stood hidden next to a huge overrun bush at the end of the fence line near the driveway so that Father could not see anyone standing there. My mother rushed my brother back to the house to find our sister and get her as fast as he could. While waiting, my mother's face and body language displayed alarm and panic. She hysterically signed to me that we had to run very fast. Her face was red, and her eyes wandered nervously around the house. A few minutes later, my brother and sister met up with us. With no time to waste, we crossed the road and ran for our lives.

There was no turning back on U.S. 12. We had no choice. My mother cried as she ran. I felt her pain. We constantly looked back in case Father came after us. My imagination got the better of me as I thought of him chasing us down or even running us over in his car.

We stopped at a neighbor's house about a mile down. My mother pled with the neighbor to take us to the police station. Concerned and without hesitation, the neighbor drove us there immediately. As soon as we arrived, my mother told me to disclose to the police everything about my father sexually abusing me.

After years of ignoring and denying me help, she finally acknowledged the sexual abuse and wanted me to confess it to the police. It had been a long time coming. My father had threatened to kill her for eleven years if she told anyone. I could tell that my mother cracked. She wanted it out in the open.

I mustered up the courage to detail to the police what my father had done to me throughout my childhood. My mother also reported his violent threats of killing all of us.

The police drove all of us back to the house because I had to interpret and translate for everyone.

Once we entered the house, my father pretended to be calm and in control because of the presence of the police officers. I did not want to be in the middle of the dispute. As I was interpreting back and forth, my father kept denying all the accusations about him. Finally, he told me to tell the police that he never had sex with me. I stared at him in disbelief. He pointed his finger at me to tell them precisely what he said. As a CODA, I felt trapped and had to interpret and relay his lies to the police. I felt betrayed as I spoke the exact words my father signed. I interpreted it without defending myself because fear gripped me. I felt my father's heavy eyes on me.

Further, his defense was that my mother was a mentally unstable lunatic and had to be on medication. He further said that she belonged in a mental institution. For the record, everything was pointed to my mother as to why the family and marriage fell apart. My mother broke down in tears in front of the police, telling them he was not telling the truth.

His dishonesty, deceit, and treachery exploited us to protect himself at all costs. It hurt me so much that he would be so defiant as to deny having sex with me in front of my face.

The police suggested my father leave the house and relocate somewhere else until the domestic dispute was resolved. My father cleverly made a move and went to live in Indiana, just over the border from where we lived in Michigan.

Through all the abuse we went through, my father got away with murder, so to speak. He never went to jail. After much questioning and investigations from government officials and law enforcement, they did not believe my story, nor my mother's. My father's tale was more convincing and had more weight than ours.

My mother began the divorce process at once. My mother, brother, sister, and I were at peace for the first time. It was a wonderful sense of freedom. I had never known what it was like to have a normal childhood without sexual abuse, except for the great memories one year when I attended boarding school in Bloomington, Indiana. It was a strange new feeling not to have my body used by my father at his every beck and call. Consequently, I still had to pick up the tab with the eleven years of the dysfunctional mess he inflicted upon me.

I started seventh grade and attended Mottville Jr. High School, several miles west of home.

My siblings continued attending special ed at their school in another nearby town.

We had visits every week from a local social worker. She checked in on us and helped us to obtain food stamps and financial means to help pay for our needs. The only thing complicated was that we did not have any transportation.

Once the cat was out of the bag, my mother's entire side of the family was relieved that my father was out of the picture for good. None of the family members liked my father.

Therefore, Uncle John and Aunt Alice would swing by often and take us to the store or pick us up to stay for the weekend at Grandpa and Grandma's house.

With my father gone, my siblings and I got into mischief. We walked about a mile down the road and stopped by a small family-owned company. We peeked through the fence at the property. People came out and inquired what our names were and where we lived. Somehow, they picked up on the fact that we were needy. It was a married couple who owned the company. They were extremely kind to us and asked if they could meet our mother. They drove us home and introduced themselves to her. She wrote on paper to communicate with them and vice versa. They offered my mother assistance with transportation and anything else she needed. My mother was delighted with the help.

Often, the couple would surprise us with bags of groceries and trays of canned foods. Then, they would check up on us, drive us to the store if we needed anything, and even invite us to their home to eat dinner.

One day, they visited and brought three bicycles for my brother, sister, and me. We were so pumped up about it. They were excited that we were excited. Their gestures of kindness helped us get through hard times. We lived way out in the country, where I would count one car that drove by every five minutes or so. Therefore, riding bikes on the road was entirely suitable.

Growing up, we never celebrated birthdays. It was so unfortunate that even when my birthday fell on that day, I never knew about it. We never celebrated it with parties, birthday cakes, or gifts. Birthdays disappeared into the calendar as if they were like any ordinary day of the year. The only holiday we celebrated was Christmas. Every year, we got jumbo coloring books and crayons. I especially liked the jumbo Crayola crayons with a special sharpener on the back of the box.

It was the first Christmas without my father. We went to Grandpa Gerry and Grandma Pearl's house. Uncle Chet, Aunt Alice, and Jane were there. Sean returned home for R&R with his new girlfriend, whom he met from the Army after being stationed in Germany.

A collage of pictures was taped up all over the right side of the living room wall next to the huge vintage black and white TV set. Most of them were pictures of Sean and Jane. Grandma was proud of Sean's photo in his military uniform. I searched everywhere to see if my brother, sister, or I were on the wall, but we weren't. Grandma had her favorites.

Sean approached me and gave me a small present wrapped in Christmas paper. I was surprised because he never gave gifts. I could not wait to find out what he got me. The excitement was overwhelming as he watched me open it.

I cried in disbelief when I saw that it was a handheld battery-operated RadioShack radio. He included a new pack of batteries. I jumped for joy and hugged him. He smiled and was pleased knowing he picked out the right gift for me because he also knew what it was like to live in silence. This was by far the best gift in the world.

After returning home, I went to the bedroom with my new radio. I closed the door and could not wait to try it out. I carefully placed the new batteries into the battery compartment and snapped the cover in its place. I pulled the antenna as far as it could go. Then, I toggled between the AM and FM stations to search for a specific station that played rock music. I listened to the radio in my father's car before, but having my portable radio was an epic moment. Once I found the station I liked, a new song I had not heard before was playing. The song was called "Let's Groove" by Earth, Wind, and Fire. It became my favorite song. I pressed the radio against my ear, and I closed my eyes. I had imagined I had a glistening disco ball that hung in the middle of my bedroom ceiling. I danced to my version of the song. My eyes were still closed as my ears took pleasure in the rhapsodies of the tune. I then went to bed and held my radio close like a stuffed toy. I was eternally grateful for it. At thirteen years old, it was the first time I ever slept well in eleven years.

CHAPTER TWELVE:

Sold and Carried Away

Mother was under so much turmoil in the middle of the divorce and her father's death in March of 1981. My grandpa Gerry's passing never affected me because he never wanted to have a relationship with me. Moreover, I thought he was an extraordinarily strange grandfather because he never once uttered a word to me, even though he could talk.

During that time, the appliance company took our stove and refrigerator because we could not make payments on them anymore. As a result, we had nothing to cook our food on and no fridge for about six months. However, we got by and ate white bread, peanut butter, and powdered milk.

―――――――――

The school year was over, and summer came. We continued to live in survival mode on a daily basis. Finally, our social worker advised my mother to move from the country to the city. Times were desperate, and we had to move to utilize the city's transit buses as a means of transportation. My mother took her advice and made plans to sell the house. She knew that we could not live there anymore.

Eventually, my mother sold the two-bedroom home for only one thousand dollars.

I remember my mother staked a garage sale sign near the road next to the other sign inscribed "House Sold." My mother, brother, sister, and I moved almost everything from our house onto the grass and driveway. The furniture, housewares, tools, and everything you could think of inside the home were now outside. I stared at the heap of stuff we had out on the driveway. The inside of the house was pretty much empty. It was too much to bear. I had grown up with much trauma; this one was just another of those episodes. It felt like a root was being pulled up from the ground.

Buyers came steadily throughout the day. So many things had much sentiment. My record player and all the record albums were sold. It was hard to see them go. I mourned and felt a stinging pain when they were sold and carried away.

The social worker gathered the four of us and our belongings into the car. I had no idea where we were going.

We arrived at an apartment complex in Kalamazoo, Michigan. We moved into a two-bedroom apartment on the first floor. It was completely furnished and decent. I had to adjust to city life since I was accustomed to rural living.

The social worker said her goodbyes as she transferred us into the hands of a new social worker named Mr. Dodge. We also were introduced to an attorney named Mr. Sullivan, who took over our case on behalf of the state. He shared that he was a Catholic, retired from the law firm, and was taking on cases to help kids in the community. He was a kind elderly man with wavy gray hair and gnarly, arthritic hands. He wore a pressed business suit and tie and drove a black BMW with off-white woolly sheepskin seat covers. He looked around our apartment and mentioned that he would work on getting us a small color TV. He stopped by from time to time to check up on us.

I started attending seventh and eighth-grade junior high school. It was not easy starting over, especially with what I had gone through. The city was so different than where I grew up. City kids wore their collars straight up. Izod was the popular brand that most students wore during that time. The Preppies, or The Preps, were a group of rich kids. There was also another group of Valley Girls who spoke slang words in every sentence. If a Valley Girl was disgusted at something, she would say, "Gag me with a pitchfork." If it were something awesome, the response would be, "Totally tubular." The list of phrases was endless.

The word "like" was used in almost every word. This was all new to me, and I wanted to feel I belonged. I started talking like a Valley Girl and was determined to get an Izod shirt at the thrift store. The only Izod available was a used red, green, white, and black striped long-sleeved shirt. Even though it looked like a Christmas shirt, I purchased it and wore it because I believed it was like a passport to fit in with the crowd. But to my chagrin, it did not work. I was poor and very homely. There was barely any extra money to buy hair products or cosmetics. I started to become a loner at school. Being in homeroom class was difficult because some students teased me about my first name. My hopes for a better life were nothing but a distant dream.

A neighbor girl named Gemma lived at the same apartment complex as I did, but she was a grade ahead of me. She was sexually active, heavily drank beer and whiskey, smoked cigarettes, and took illegal drugs. She wore a leather jacket with tight Jordache jeans every day. Gemma wore lots of makeup, and her hair was like Farrah Fawcett from the TV show *Charlie's Angels.*

I believed she took pity on me and took me under her wing even though I felt uncomfortable with her sex and drug addictions. Gemma and I had no other friends. We knew we were outcasts; therefore, we became besties. She never forced me to do drugs or to engage in other illegal dealings. She just wanted my friendship.

Gemma was so generous to let me borrow her hairdryer. It was my first time using it. She taught me how to use a curling iron on my hair. She shared her clothes, hair products, and makeup. Gemma was like a sister and helped transform me from a country to a city girl.

Eventually, boys in my school and even college guys used me for one-night stands. I wanted to date, but it seemed it was not on their radar. I did not know any better. Neither my mother nor father helped instruct me about puberty and what I would face during my teenage years.

My mother and I went to a local Supercenter Store to buy a new pair of shoes because my feet outgrew my other pair. Gemma would have been willing to share her shoes with me, but we wore different sizes. Therefore, I asked my mother if I could purchase a pair of light blue Nike tennis shoes like Gemma's. They had a dark blue swoosh on them. Moreover, I explained to my mother that I could wear them with everything for school and gym class. She ignored me and pulled out a pair of fake leather moccasin slippers. I told her I did not like them and explained in sign language that they were slippers for wearing around the home. She resisted and told me to try them on. I hesitated and slipped them on to show her. She grabbed them and threw them into the cart. I explained to my mother that I could not run or do exercises in the school gym with slippers on. She ignored my pleas.

I put the slippers on and left the apartment on my way to the bus stop. There were no protective rubber soles underneath them. It felt like I was wearing socks outside without shoes. I could feel the pebbles under my feet. It was very uncomfortable that I had to redirect my attention to where I was walking to avoid stepping on anything in my path. I approached the bus stop but avoided the crowd so they could not see my slippers. Isolating myself was the only remedy to avoid being teased. I wished that Gemma and I were in the same grade. Low self-worth and loneliness were my constant companions in school.

A couple of months later, we had a scheduled court session. Honestly, I had no idea what we were doing at the courthouse. I figured it was just a routine evaluation. Mr. Dodge and Mr. Sullivan were there. A sign language interpreter was hired to assist in translating for my mother. Everything looked formal, with a judge sitting across from where I was with my mother, brother, and sister in the courtroom. I listened to Mr. Sullivan and Mr. Dodge explain our situation to the judge. It was not long until the judge declared that my mother was mentally unstable and emotionally unfit to care for my siblings and me. My mother had spiraled out of control mentally the past year ever since the social services did not believe her story or mine. My mother risked everything and thought we would get justice for what my father did to us, yet she became the scapegoat and was blamed for the family breakdown. She completely flipped mentally into another dimension. I noticed her decline rapidly that past year. She was recommended to see a psychologist. I could not understand why my father did not appear in court and got away with everything. It felt like the whole justice system was rigged. No one believed us.

The judge decreed that my twin siblings and I would be separated into different foster homes. I would not see my siblings again for a long time. When it was decided that I would be sent to foster care, I watched my mother jump for joy, exclaiming in sign language, "I'm free, I'm free, I'm free." She was laughing and dancing in the middle of the courtroom with her hands up high and clapping everywhere. She looked so happy. It was so confusing to me. I could not believe what I was witnessing. *My mother does not want me anymore?* I thought. I left the courtroom and sat outside the hallway, sobbing loudly and uncontrollably with my hands over my head. My brother and sister joined me in unison. Our cries echoed throughout the halls of the broken justice system. Our screams were never heard.

The social worker, the judge, and the lawyer acted as if it was business as usual. It appeared that they had conducted this so many times without showing compassion. My mother mirrored them and betrayed my brother, sister, and me. She did not hug us or say, "I love you," before we all went our separate ways. It felt as if she sold us like garage sale items. We were sold and carried away, never to return.

CHAPTER THIRTEEN:

The Night Jesus Knocked at the Door

I could not adjust emotionally when I moved from one home to the next. That went the same for school. I dreaded changing schools, which meant starting all over again. Mr. Dodge drove me to my new foster home that afternoon. I ended up living with the Griswold family. They lived in a rough and dangerous neighborhood in Kalamazoo. Their house was approximately four hundred yards near a train track. Each day, trains bolted past the house and the surrounding communities with thunderous blasts from the horn as a warning before passing the road where the train track had crossed. The entire house shook as if an earthquake struck the area.

The family was originally from Georgia and spoke in a Southern twang. The foster father worked at an automotive plant, and I barely saw him because he worked many hours. The foster mother took in temporary and permanent foster children and teens. Eventually, I became one of their permanent ones. The youth were constantly in and out of that home as the state-run foster care system was trying to shuffle them around, trying to find homes for them. I remember a drug addict who was so high that he did not last there even for a few hours. He was a violent teenager and punched my nose for no apparent reason. I was knocked out cold. The authorities immediately removed him because no one felt safe with him around the home.

It was my first time living with a family that spoke. I felt out of place, especially when I grew up in silence my whole childhood for fourteen years. This time, it was different. I still communicated in sign language with my hands at the foster home. I could not stop moving them. People noted it with strange looks and would tell me I moved my hands too much. That was my world. I was thrust into this family where everyone had a voiced opinion attached with a swear word in every sentence, talking super loud in their pronounced Southern drawl. I was afraid the whole time I lived there.

Mrs. Griswold was a frail lady with sunken eyes. She had an icy-cold personality and looked like a witch from *The Wizard of Oz*. I barely saw her eat any food. On average, she drank a dozen cups of coffee and smoked a box of cigarettes every day. She had a best friend named Paisley, whom I liked very much. She had dark, beautiful, naturally curly hair and brown eyes and weighed over 250 pounds. Paisley came religiously every morning and stayed there until late afternoon. She was nicer to me than Mrs. Griswold. The only thing these ladies had in common was drinking coffee, smoking cigarettes, and gossiping at the kitchen table about anything and anyone.

I tried to do my very best to please the foster family. Mrs. Griswold said that the only reason I was living there was so that she would get a paycheck. It cut me like a knife to hear that. Her unkind actions and words rang loud enough for me to understand that she did not care about me. As a foster mother, she never took the time to help make a difference in my life. I was treated as a case. Every child who went through Mrs. Griswold's home was just a business transaction to put money into her pocket.

———————————

Mr. Dodge checked in very often and met with Mrs. Griswold on how I was progressing. He set up appointments for me to see a psychologist once a week. I honestly hated it. I moved from one psychologist to the next. One made me very uncomfortable, and all she did was sit in her chair and stare at me for an entire hour. It was a strange method, and I requested never to see her again.

Mr. Sullivan stopped by about once every month. I was only in eighth grade and was still receiving Social Security checks because of my father's retirement and disability. It was a blessing in disguise to receive financial help. Mr. Sullivan helped set up an account at the bank to have it manually deposited until I reached the age of eighteen.

I asked Mr. Sullivan if I could get braces with my money because my teeth were extremely crooked. He agreed that it was based on need and, therefore, took the time to find an orthodontist in the local area. He drove me to my first appointment to help with the initial consultation and payment plan. After that, I took the city transit bus to my monthly appointments.

The one friend I had for consolation was my foster sister, Roxanne. She lived at the Griswolds' home as their permanent foster child because her father sexually abused her. We had much in common. We were both fourteen years old and in the eighth grade. We were considered scum at school. We both had similar misfortunes, yet we became good friends. She had terrible acne and greasy, dirty blonde hair, yet she was a nice girl. I would have run away from that home if it were not for Roxanne.

I'll never forget New Year's Eve 1983. I remember the cold, blustery winter snowfall in Parchment, Michigan. Roxanne and I took the city transit bus and visited her aunt and uncle's house for the weekend. Roxanne had often visited them and stayed over on the weekends. Since it was a holiday, I was invited.

Out of the blue, there was a knock on the door. It was late in the evening. My mind raced about who it would be at that late hour. It was snowing steadily, and temps fell below freezing.

Roxanne's aunt opened the front door. A Baptist pastor was paying a visit from a local church in the area. The pastor asked if he could come in and share some things from the Bible with us. Gladly, Roxanne's aunt and uncle led him into the dining room. As we all joined him at the table, he read Scripture verses and explained the gospel of Jesus Christ.

Memories flooded my mind when I went to church with the three strangers. I remember being excited when there was a knock on the front door every Sunday. The strangers picked me up to take me to their church. I liked the strangers and their God. I wanted their God to be my God.

I looked at the pastor, who reminded me much like the strangers from my past. As he read the scriptures, I was moved and drawn in my spirit, not because of what he shared but because I knew Jesus was in the room. Everyone felt His presence, too. We were all overcome with God's love and grace as tears of repentance poured out, and we confessed with our mouths that Jesus Christ was our Lord and Savior. I realized then that it was not just the pastor alone who made all this effort to come, nor the strangers from my past, but it was Jesus who came to visit. I let Jesus into my heart that very night.

The pastor invited us to church service the next day to be baptized. The last time I had gone to church with the three strangers was when I was just a little girl. The opportunity finally came for me to go.

The next morning, on New Year's Day, we all geared up with extra clothes for our baptism. The cold weather was not going to stop us from going. So, we loaded into the car, drove to church, and got baptized.

CHAPTER FOURTEEN:

Sweet and Sour Sixteen

I took the city bus to visit my mother in downtown Kalamazoo, Michigan. Even though I still felt rejected by her not wanting me, I still loved and missed her. Mr. Dodge explained that my mother would meet me downtown on the main street, where the city buses often stopped. I got off the bus and saw my mother standing on the sidewalk. City streets were bustling with people that day. I asked her why we had to meet here and not at her apartment. She said that she did not live there anymore. She explained that she wandered on these streets all day because the homeless shelter was closed during the day and only reopened in the evenings. The shelter offered hot dinners and a bed to sleep on every night.

I was dazed and confused by what she said and could not believe what she told me. *My mother is homeless?* I thought. *If she was in the state's care, why was she homeless?* Her deaf family was in Indiana, and they could have helped her. But they didn't. Mother acted as though she was happy with her situation, making it more difficult for me to process in my mind.

I hoped my mother would have found a better life and made good choices away from Father, but she chose this life.

Mother grew more and more garrulous as time went on. She did not know when to stop. I looked at her with exhaustion and watched her hands sign everything that went through her mind, and then she would repeat it all over again. It was like listening to a broken LP record. She went on and on about a psychologist whose name was Dr. Brown. Her smile was enough for me to know that she liked this man. She went into imaginary prolix sex sagas about him. I became uncomfortable and tried to change the subject, but she would never let me have a word in edgewise.

My mother and I approached the intersection. Many people stood and waited to cross the street. The crosswalk sign finally appeared, and the cars stopped at the red light. We walked quickly with the other pedestrians. Mother behaved in a strange way I had never seen before. Out of nowhere, she ran right up in front of a car, raised both hands, and halted the driver not to move the car. Of course, the car never moved because it was at a stoplight. Then, my mother sounded out with a loud shrill and gestured with her finger at the driver to look at the red light. The driver's face looked perplexed. Then she jumped up and down, ran wildly to the next car, and repeated the same scenario. I could not believe what I witnessed. I was so embarrassed by her bizarre behavior that I kept walking, pretending I did not know her. This was all new to me.

I observed the pedestrians as they looked at her with wonder or amusement. This was not the same mother I knew before. I knew that my father had destroyed her mental self-image, but I never imagined that it would take it beyond the boundaries of normalcy and sanity.

Since then, my mother and I slowly drifted apart even though we never had a typical mother-and-daughter relationship. I finally made a conscious decision to close that chapter in my life. It felt wasted after all the years I had cared for her throughout my childhood. I had hopeful and high expectations that we would have an excellent relationship, but she had made the wrong choices and got involved with men like my father. I would not honor that, so I decided not to have any part of it anymore. That relationship was gone and lost forever. All I could do was love her from a distance and pray for her. Being a teenager, I had to figure out things on my own.

In 1984, I was going to turn sweet sixteen. It was a huge deal for teenage girls. I had thought that perhaps Mrs. Griswold would do something special for me on my birthday. Then, one day, it did happen; she brought out a humongous box all wrapped up. I was so excited and taken aback by her generosity for such a huge gift. The box stood about six feet tall. I looked up at it, and I was gleaming with joy. It was just her and me in the kitchen. I carefully took the wrapping paper off and then opened the box. I took the item out and placed it on the linoleum kitchen floor. I stared at it, puzzled, and then Mrs. Griswold laughed. I did not understand what was so funny. I tried to muster up the humiliation of it all and then kindly said, "Thank you, Mrs. Griswold," despite her prank, especially on my sixteenth birthday. I brought the six-foot wooden coat rack to my bedroom and stared at it for a long time. I wondered what made her buy it for me and why she did it. My heart was hurt by what she did. I kept it to myself and would never forget that prank. My sweet sixteen turned into a sour sixteen. I did not own many coats to warrant a coat rack. I only owned one jacket.

Mr. Sullivan picked me up to spend the afternoon washing his black BMW outside his driveway. He lived in the wealthy area of Kalamazoo on Bronson Boulevard. His wife was there but did not welcome me, nor was she very friendly. It did not seem as though Mr. Sullivan and his wife were on friendly terms, or perhaps she did not like foster children. After we washed the car, we spun it around the block because it helped air dry the vehicle. We returned to his house and finished drying it with clean towels.

Shortly after, we went back inside his house and had lunch. Mr. Sullivan was a good conversationalist and was never dull. After a month, he picked me up, and we had lunch at his house again. His wife still avoided me like the plague. He drove me back to drop me off at the Griswolds' house. Then, after about another month, Mr. Sullivan picked me up again for lunch. We arrived, and he prepared sandwiches and delicious warm soup.

He was chatty as usual when, for some odd reason, he had an unusual request and asked me to pet him.

I did not know what he meant by that. I looked at him in confusion. He went on to explain that his wife was not home. He said he and I were alone and invited me to his bedroom. With his friendly manner, he calmly explained to me that it was okay to pet and stroke each other in bed. He said it was completely harmless and fun. When he said that, I gasped. I told him I wanted to go back to the Griswolds' house.

He was surprised by my answer and calmly told me not to tell anyone what he said because he said he would lose his law license. I did not care if he lost his license; I just wanted to get away from this old, sick man.

The car trip back to my foster home was silent and uncomfortable. He was calm in his manner with no remorse. He reminded me again not to share this with anyone. I did not respond to him. I had trusted this man explicitly as one of my guardians through the government's state-run foster care system. He had deceived me into thinking I was safe with him.

In tenth grade, I dated a guy named David. His mom, Patty, and I got along well. She was a Christian woman. She was much nicer than Mrs. Griswold and my biological mother put together. She knew the dire situation that I was living in.

She told me she was acquainted with a woman who lived in another town next to hers located on the outskirts of Kalamazoo. Patty mentioned that the woman only took in teenage girls and wondered if I would be interested in transferring under her care. I trusted her completely and gave her my consent to make further inquiries about the matter.

To make a long story short, the foster mother who lived near Patty was Ele Baxter. Unfortunately, I received a reply from Patty that Ele was not taking in any more girls. As a former foster mother, she had taken in approximately fifteen girls and closed that chapter in her life. Even though Ele told Patty she was not doing foster care anymore, Ele said she would think about it. After much thought, Ele said she would gladly interview me before making a final decision. She went through the Youth for Christ foster care and had them work out something with Mr. Dodge to set up an interview. He picked me up and took me to Ele's house to be interviewed one day. A few days later, after much consideration, I was notified by Mr. Dodge that Ele wanted to take me in to live with her. I was elated.

I packed my belongings and waited at the front door for Ele. With a haughty look, Mrs. Griswold sat at the kitchen table and smoked her cigarette in her usual place.

Ele's car pulled up in front of the Griswolds' house. After living there for about three years, I was relieved to move out of the home. Ele walked up to the front door and politely greeted Mrs. Griswold, who never got up from her chair but gave Ele a cold greeting while puffing her cigarette. Ele took the high road. She was a cheerful and confident woman. She asked me if I was ready to go. I nodded my head with a big "Yes!"

The ride with Ele on the way to her home felt nerve-racking at first, but I was excited at the same time. We arrived in the small village of Augusta. I moved in with Ele at sixteen in the summer of 1985. Ele showed me around the home and my bedroom upstairs. It was a good adjustment period, especially because it was about a couple of months before school started. Ele was a devout and sincere Christian lady who attended a very old Methodist church in town. She was heavily involved in church activities and was the pianist almost every Sunday. Ele told me that Harriet Tubman had come to that church as one of her routes during the Underground of the Civil War era. She had done these rescue missions multiple times, helping enslaved people start a new life.

Perhaps landing in this town and into Ele's care, who was like the modern-day Harriet, was a sign of my new beginning and freedom.

Ele was on her own, yet she was a very successful woman. She was a pharmacist and owned her pharmacy and grocery store. She also was the mayor of Augusta.

I will never forget the decorative license plate she placed in front of her brand-new light powder blue Buick. It said, "Ask Your Pharmacist, She Knows Everything."

Even though I was supposed to be her last foster child, she took in another girl. Her name was Allison. She and I were the same age and in the same grade. We're still friends to this day.

Ele introduced me to a girl named Jackie Kelley at the church. Jackie was in the same grade as I was. We became fast friends and hung out a lot that summer. One day, just a few weeks before entering the new high school, Jackie told me to sit down because she had something important that she wanted to talk to me about. I gave her a puzzled look and wondered what she would say. She proceeded, "You have to change your first name."

Her urgent plea surprised me, but the more I thought about it, the more I agreed with her. The awareness of it was like a light switch turned on. I was so used to and accustomed to being named "Thelma" that I did not think more about it. I had gotten used to being teased by classmates. I never dreamed I had a right to choose, let alone change my name. It was the first time that I had sensed freedom. I never learned what it was like to be free. I grew up shackled and in the clutches of my father and mother. They had defined me. Jackie was one of those friends trying to save me from being teased. She said that if I changed my name, everyone at the new school would never know my former name. It would be a fresh new start.

I was so hesitant at first but was excited about this idea. She asked me what I liked for a first name. I told her names like Lisa, Amy, and Michelle. Jackie shook her head in disagreement and said, "No, it does not fit you." Then, immediately, she blurted out a name that I now legally own… "I know! Your new name will be Morgan." I gasped and told her I felt insignificant having a name like that. I loved her suggestion, but I settled for a simpler name. Jackie would not have it. She told me she would call me Morgan, and from that day on, she never stopped calling me by that new name. She was set and determined.

The name change took on a new effect in my life right away. That moment felt like I was "turning over a new leaf." I told Ele about my new name. She supported the idea and has called me "Morgan" since then.

Mr. Sullivan, who had taken care of my case since I started foster care, said he would take me to the courthouse and draw me up an official legal name change document. It was a special moment. He asked if I wanted to change my middle name, but I kept "Jean" because it was a French name for John. It was a Bible name, and I wanted to keep it because John the Beloved was close and near and dear to Jesus's heart.

I pondered and considered that this new name would be my belated sweet sixteenth birthday present. God was so good to bless me with the best gift ever.

Even though Mr. Sullivan helped with the name change, I felt he did it to cover up his past sexual advances toward me. I have always noticed that Ele did not like him very much. It was the last time Mr. Sullivan would ever have connections with me. Since Ele took me under her wings, he left the picture for good. I felt safe living in a Christian home and under the protection of Youth for Christ. I experienced living in both the state-run foster care and Christian foster care systems. The latter was way better.

Ele took those last two years of my high school career and crammed everything she could possibly think of to give me experiences and the best memories ever.

Ele had put so much time and effort into helping me to be a successful person. She did not mind at all, either! She constantly reminded me that "ain't" was not a word and told me to sit up straight and put my shoulders back because her adage was, "If you got it, flaunt it!" Looking back, I sure appreciate everything that she taught me.

Ele's elderly parents often visited from time to time. We had dinner together. Her mother was very affluent in English as she was an English teacher back in the day. After eating dinner, I distinctly remember her saying in a distinct, proper, and polite manner, "My sofonsifation is sofonsified." I totally did not get what she was talking about. Ele explained to me that her mother loved to invent words. She translated her mom's big words for me; all it meant was, "My stomach is full."

I had experienced blessings from God in those two years living with Ele, which generally would be spread over many years. I read in the Bible about Jesus's first public miracle, how He produced the best quality wine from water at the wedding feast of Cana, which would have taken so many years to do. I had experienced the God of the Bible in my life, who accelerated natural laws and accomplished dreams faster than I thought possible.

Ele took me and Allison on vacation to Mackinac Island. She also took me to Houston, Texas. It was my first time flying in an airplane. I had never seen a world so big before. We went to NASA, the Gulf of Mexico, a rodeo, and experienced a variety of seafood. Ele also sent me to church camp and signed me up to go to Mexico with a missionary team.

Her expertise as a pharmacist taught me how to take care of myself. She gave me Lomotil tablets in case I got Montezuma's Revenge on that mission trip. Unfortunately, I caught it and was very ill, but with her help and advice, I was able to take care of myself during that trip back home.

Ele always knew how to keep me out of trouble. I got into a lot of mischief. She did not know over half of what I did behind her back. Maybe she knew. But even if she did, she always showed me love and grace. When she and her family had to go somewhere for an event, she kept me occupied with things to do to stay out of trouble.

In one of those instances, I had to sew a simple straight stitch project to prevent drafts from entering the front door. I had no choice because I had to live by the rules in the house, or I would be grounded. Ele gave me basic house rules and things to do to avoid being idle. It helped me to stay out of trouble for the most part. I did not know it then, but she did it because she cared.

Ele introduced me to latch hook rugs and cross-stitching. It inspired creativity, and I never got tired of making many handmade projects.

In 1986, just before my senior year, I worked at a cemetery. It was my first summer job. The minimum wage was $3.35 per hour. Since Ele was the mayor of Augusta, I was the chosen candidate for the job. My job was to pull weeds around every headstone in that spooky cemetery. I was terrified of working there all alone. I had thoughts of ghosts appearing out of the shadows behind those stones.

Day by day, I groomed the cemetery grounds. I remember one time in the middle of a beautiful summer day, as I was pulling weeds around a particular giant headstone, when, out of the blue, I heard a terrifying morbid scream. I froze in my tracks and raised the garden tool in my hand as my only weapon. The sound was getting closer and closer, so I decided to make a run for it. I stayed hidden behind the headstone, and just when I was about to run away, a figure jumped out from behind a monumental gravestone and howled at me. I screamed and felt like my eyeballs flew out of my sockets. It was my former high school boyfriend, David.

In the middle of the summer, my job at the cemetery ended abruptly with a bad case of poison ivy! I was glad not to work at the cemetery but was not happy to suffer the itching all over my hands and body. Ele knew what to use for my itch. Benadryl, Calamine lotion, and other meds became my best friends. I then started working inside the township hall, where Ele served as mayor. She pulled out paper scrolls of cemetery plot maps that looked ancient and tattered. She supplied me with pencils, erasers, pens, markers, a ruler, and new rolls of crisp, white paper. I drew rectangles, then wrote every buried person's name next to them, and accurately added the plot location from the old maps.

At Halloween time, Ele went all out. She prepared a fantastic party for me and told me to invite friends I had met at summer camp. She had everything planned out and decorated the home. During the party, Ele had all of us teenagers sit in a circle in the dark. We all sat around listening to her share scary stories. Afterward, we passed around a bowl in the dark and had to reach in with one hand to feel a brain. It was creepy and slimy. We found out later that it was just spaghetti noodles and Jell-O gelatin.

During my senior year in high school, Ele taught me the importance of college. She instructed me, "You never know what will happen in the future," as she always reminded me. She shared with me her marriage devastation and divorce. Ele was incredibly thankful for having a college degree to provide for herself financially. She gave me insight, wisdom, and direction. She helped me apply for financial aid to attend Kellogg Community College (a.k.a. Cornflake U). She helped me find a potential grant. Ele drove me to an interview and pushed me to talk with the board and share my story and why I needed it. They nominated me and gave me the financial means to help fund my first year at college.

Ele and I practiced a hymn song to perform at church together. She wanted me to sing "In the Garden" while she played the piano. We practiced for about a month together. She was so patiently instructive in helping me with the song. When that Sunday came around to perform, I told Ele I was afraid to sing in front of people and did not feel comfortable doing it. Ele never showed any anger, nor was she upset at all. She smiled at me and looked at me with an understanding look and said that we would sing it perhaps another time.

CHAPTER FIFTEEN:

A Father's Love for a Fatherless Father

It was mid-winter during the new year in 1990; I entered on a trial basis that year at Asbury College in Kentucky. I was not supposed to be accepted at the college because of my poor credentials. My journey as a young woman was like a roller coaster as I searched for identity and true purpose. It seemed that almost everything was a struggle. I was new, and as I compared myself to many other college students, I felt that I was the runt of the litter. All my college mates had parents, affluence, and everything else going for them. It was a private Christian college, and the tuition was vastly expensive. Their families, churches, and other supporters paid their college tuition. Being accepted on a trial basis did not help me gain any momentum, especially when I did not have any financial support or even any superior academics to be deemed worthy of attending there. The only reason I went there was because of a missionary's suggestion. All I did was ask if there were any future missionary trips. The missionary pushed me to attend the Christian college and used his well-known influence in the town to help me gain access there, but eventually, it caused me to be in debt.

I was not used to being around these people who seemed to have it all together. I felt outside the circle. As a born-again Christian, I tried blending in and talking with students at lunchtime. It was futile. It was apparent what types of people were in each section of the lunchroom. It was no different than when I was in public high school. There were many cliques. Being a newborn Christian brought perspective to me as I observed most students who grew up their whole lives influenced by their Christian upbringing. They appeared to have everything together with no care in the world. The students were very well dressed. There was a dress code that I did not like very much. All the women had to wear skirts. I never entirely understood why women suffered through the cold winter temperatures wearing them. I only had two skirts to my name. One was a makeshift one that I made by hand. It would do.

Eventually, I became friends with several people through my college roommate. We were instant friends and did everything together. One time, we went to the Kentucky River. We packed into the car with our beach towels hanging around our necks. We made our way there through narrow, twisty roads. There were beautiful, natural, massive rock formations everywhere I looked. Finally, we arrived at the spot where we would go cliff jumping. As we arrived, many other college students were plunging into the river. We took our shoes off before we approached the edge of the cliff. I was shocked that the river was fifty-five feet from where I stood. There was a specific spot where everyone jumped into the water. Other areas were hazardous because a story was circulated about a person who jumped off a cliff nearby and crashed onto boulders of rocks unseen just a few feet underwater. I watched to make sure it was safe. If everyone could do it, so could I. I was never the type who said no to new adventures. It only came once in a lifetime. So, I took the plunge.

It was the last day of classes. The once-buzzing college campus rapidly became deadly silent, with only a few students left roaming around. Most of the students flew or drove home or elsewhere for the summer. My college mates lived in various states across the nation and other countries around the globe. Only a handful of students stayed on for summer classes or worked on campus. I did the latter. There was no home for me to go back to. So, I signed up for summer work alongside other college and seminary students to clean the dorms and resident housing while the other crews did maintenance and repairs to prepare it for the next school year.

Cleaning the dorm rooms, kitchenettes, and bathrooms was tedious. Bathrooms were my least favorite because the shower stalls were plagued by mold and mildew. We used our elbow grease to scour the tiles and grout until they were clean. Then, one of the guys impulsively had a great idea. He brought a long green outdoor water hose to the third floor. We watched him as he found a way to attach the hose to a water source in the kitchenette. He turned the water on and followed the hose trail leading him back to the bathroom. Other students and I watched the guy pick up the hose. He aimed it toward the tiles inside the shower stall, twisted the sprayer nozzle slowly on the jet setting, and instantly, the water pressure blew black bits of mold off. We all evacuated quickly from the backfire as we cheered and laughed at the guy drenched with water and covered with the black moldy bits that peppered his body. This made our summer cleaning job a whole lot of fun together.

I closed my Bible after I read Joel Chapter Two about God restoring the years that the locusts had eaten. I had this mental image of locusts eating all the leaves, grass, and flowers, leaving an entire landscape barren. Tears started to well up in my eyes because it triggered thoughts about what my father and mother had done to me in the past. They had stolen my childhood. They were like those locusts that destroyed everything I ever hoped for as a child. I wanted a dad and a mom. I wanted a family that I could call home. The one thing that gave me hope was Joel's prophecy that God would restore the years that the locusts had eaten. Ever since I saw the word *restore*, it has been my yearning hope to see it come to pass. I asked God specifically to restore my virginity.

I left my dorm room and walked down the barren hallway where the summer sun peeked in through the window from the end of the hallway. There was not a soul anywhere. I let out a scream, "God, where are you?" There was nothing but deadly silence in the building. I felt as though I was trapped and surrounded by a cloud of darkness. Past traumatic scenes haunted me almost daily, and I could not shake them off. They clung to me like a monkey on my back. It was like watching reruns of a movie, and I could not turn the switch off. It felt real every time I replayed the scenes in my mind. I allowed them to keep me in a cycle of despair. The memories were an ash heap that I wallowed in day and night. They just would not go away. I honestly wanted to be unchained from everything and everyone from my past. I was young and genuinely did not understand God. I had mixed views of Him yet still desired to be near Him.

One night, on a crisp and cool evening, I walked across the street to the seminary, where I attended an outdoor event gathering. I believe it had something to do with a project for deaf people in the community. Afterward, an international student from India introduced himself to me. His name was Richard Samuel. We became instant friends. He attended seminary and had plans to return to India to do mission work helping destitute widows, abandoned children, and abused teens. Richard was a godsend as I shared my struggles and wept bitterly, trying to make sense of everything in my life. He opened the Bible and read verses to comfort me. That was how he helped me. He always turned to the Bible as the source for help and read to me until I had calmed down. Afterward, he prayed and spoke reassuringly, "Morgie, you're never alone."

Thoughts about forgiving my father came from time to time. Matters of the heart needed to be brought to the surface. I was afraid that the idea of seeing him would make it even more difficult for me to forgive him. The pressure built up inside me, and I felt it was time to visit my father. I had not seen him for many years since my parents' divorce. I did not know how to approach my father about it. I was going to show up and let fate take its course.

It was Father's Day weekend in June of 1991. I was twenty-two years old. I took a six-hour road trip to my father's house north of Indiana, which was close to the border of Michigan. He was taken aback with wide-eyed astonishment when I arrived at his house. To my surprise, my visit made him tremble. His demeanor was the opposite of what I had known of him as a child. He was in his late seventies. I could see the guilt written all over his face. His facial expressions and body language showed me he was unsure why I showed up.

I paid this visit of my own volition. It was quiet inside the house. The deaf silence brought memories as I was taking it all in. My senses were heightened at the familiarity of it all.

As I turned to look at my father, I also sensed remorse and regret, and his face showed complete sadness. I could tell from what I gathered that my father was living a life of shame and defeat. My brother and sister walked downstairs. I greeted them and asked if we could sit down. My brother and sister sat on either side of me on the couch. My father sat opposite me on his chair. I communicated in sign language and brought up the past sexual abuse and neglect he committed against my will as a little girl and for other violations against my brother and sister. He did not let me finish the rest of my thoughts as he bolted straight from the chair and ambled slowly to the front screen door. I had said enough that he got the point. He put both hands down into the deep side pockets of his pants and looked outside from where he stood. He never moved and looked like a frozen statue for about seven minutes.

I sat patiently and waited until he was ready to talk. As a child, I remember he always walked up to the living room window every day and stared out in contemplation, so I knew he was processing all this in his mind.

Shortly after, he returned and sat down on the chair. He had tears in his eyes. I sensed that he had carried this guilt and burden for many years. Undoubtedly, he wondered for many years about my whereabouts and what I was doing. He did not know what to say, but his tears and brokenness were enough for me to see that he was sorry. He did not apologize, but that was not the point of my visit.

I looked at his face and said, "I forgive you and love you." He wept in tears when I signed those words. Then, I shared with my father that I was a Christian and how I was transformed and grew spiritually. I told him I felt weights lifted off me when I accepted Jesus into my life. I told him that I was not perfect and was still in the process of healing. I admitted to him that I did not completely understand the Bible but that I had experienced transformation from my decision to follow Jesus. I explained the gospel effortlessly and very simply so he could understand it. He was taking in all that I shared. I then asked him if he wanted to invite Jesus into his heart. Without hesitation, he nodded his head with a "yes." I helped him to pray a simple prayer, and he received Jesus into his life that day. We were in tears, and we hugged. I could tell that my father was set free from carrying so much guilt and weight in his life.

Forgiving my father was the best decision I ever made, and it gave me freedom to move forward with my life.

I left that day to go back to Kentucky. I did not know it then, but that was the last time I would ever see my father.

It was 1992, just a year after I last saw my father. I moved out of the country to live in Guatemala, Central America. It was my first year attending seminary. Classes were from February through October. In the middle of July, while I was in the library concentrating on my studies, I was interrupted and notified of grave news about my father. He was in the hospital dying. I stopped everything and walked directly to the small chapel. I was by myself and began wailing and crying aloud intensely. I did not care what people thought. I prayed that God would pour His love and grace upon him, be with him, and help him through his last hours of life. I was 2,700 miles away, but I knew my "Abba" Father was close to my father. The Holy Spirit was moving inside me with tears and groans of intercession in such a way that I cannot explain it.

I had no money to fly back to the United States to visit my father at the hospital. A missionary woman helped me and called a church where my mother went. It was not during work or church hours. A secretary picked up the phone and explained to the missionary that no one ever goes to the church building at that hour. The secretary said she only went there because she forgot something and would get it quickly, leave, and lock it up. When she went inside, the phone rang, and she answered it. The missionary explained to the secretary my situation. The secretary said that because the timing of the call was precisely when she arrived, she knew this was supernatural. She bought me a round-trip plane ticket.

It was a miracle. That was not random; that was an act of God. Just when I got all packed up and ready to fly back to the United States, the missionary received a call from the doctor at the hospital that my father had passed away. The doctor told her that he died peacefully with no struggle. She said it was a good sign that he had gone to be with the Lord. I was thankful he died peacefully, knowing God heard my cries and prayers.

I boarded the plane to the United States and was picked up by the King family, who also lived in Indiana, about an hour from where my father lived. Their hospitality was exemplary. They loaned me their Jeep so I could take care of my father's funeral arrangements. Unbeknownst to me, the King family were funeral directors and owned their own funeral home. They did so many random acts of kindness for me. I will never forget one moment when Mr. King showed me in the Scriptures how Jesus healed all people everywhere He went. He told me that Jesus could deliver my future children from being deaf-mute. He prayed for me and all of my future children and their children. He blessed my womb so no deaf spirit would claim any right over my family line.

When I arrived at my father's house, I was told I was responsible for my father's funeral arrangements. I gave 100 percent of everything in the house to my twin deaf brother and sister so they could start a new life independently. I went to the bank to close my father's account and use whatever money was there to help pay his funeral expenses. There were only five dollars in his savings account. The bank teller closed my father's account and gave me the five-dollar bill. I felt embarrassed in front of the bank teller that the five dollars were the only money left in my father's name. I left the bank and sat in the car to pray to

God for a miracle concerning my father's funeral expenses. I headed directly to the funeral home.

I arrived with the five dollars in my hand. A funeral attendant sat behind a desk. I explained my dilemma and implored him that I would make monthly payments. He smiled calmly and said that all the details were handled and that I did not have to pay a cent. I stared at the attendant with astonishment and disbelief. I thanked him and gave him the five dollars anyway. He said a private viewing was set up for me to visit with my father in a room and a public viewing with family and friends that evening. He led me to a room where my father was lying in a coffin, dressed in a suit and tie. The room had flowers everywhere; it was beautiful. I was amazed at all this and wondered who helped pay for my father's funeral arrangements. I approached my father's lifeless form, expecting him to open his eyes. This was the second time in my entire life that I had ever seen a dead person. The whole experience was surreal to me. I stayed in the room for about thirty minutes. I was in a state of shock. I could not process the fact that he was dead. I was used to stone silence with deaf people, but not in a silent room with dead people. I did not know what to say or think while standing in the room with him alone.

The fact that my father's funeral expenses were paid for was another miracle from God. It confirmed to me that my father was with Jesus. God did not leave any details out.

On the day of the funeral, my brother approached me and told me that Father had wanted to see me desperately before he died. My brother stood by his bedside, and then father, signed with his hands, said, "Tell Thelma to please forgive me for everything I did to her." He closed his eyes as his hands fell gently onto his heart.

After my brother relayed the message, I was overjoyed that God had been working in my father's heart the past year after telling him I forgave and loved him.

Seeing God's love and grace poured out to a man who did not deserve it and had destroyed my childhood took my breath away. I believe that he had an incredible entrance to heaven. God showed me His true nature of what a father is like in John 14:7–11, saying,

> If you had known Me, you would also have known My Father. From now on, you know Him and have seen Him. Philip said to Him, Lord, cause us to see the Father, and we shall be satisfied. Jesus replied, Have I been with all of you for so long a time, and do you not recognize and know Me yet, Philip? Anyone who has seen Me has seen the Father. How can you say then, Show us the Father? Do you not believe that I am in the Father, and that the Father is in Me? What I am telling you I do not say on my own authority and of My own accord, but the Father who lives continually in Me does the works. Believe Me that I am in the Father and the Father in Me; or else believe Me for the sake of the very works themselves.
>
> — John 14:7–11

Jesus is full of love, grace, mercy, and compassion. There-fore, regardless of what my father did to me, I chose to forgive him and lead him to Christ so that he could also experience and receive love from God the Father. You see, my father had never known his birth father. He was fatherless.

Luke 15:11–32 is a beautiful story about the prodigal son. The prodigal son asks his father to give him his inheritance. "Prodigal" means "drive away and wasteful." So, the son spent all the money on prostitutes and wild living. The father is a type of God Himself. After the son spent all his money, he worked feeding pigs. He was so hungry that he said his father's servants ate better than him. He already planned to tell his father that he'd work as one of his servants to earn his bread. He only thought about food. The father saw his son coming from a long distance away and felt compassion for him.

The son had dishonored his father, yet the father had compassion. That is how God demonstrates Himself to a prodigal. God initiated love for my father even though he did not deserve it. It was not my love; it was from God the Father. Love is what brings repentance. It's not the other way around. It's not repenting first, and then you will receive love. That is not God's heart in this story. When the father ran to his son, he hugged and kissed him. The father initiated first. God runs to you! Christians have a problem with this because they believe you must repent first before receiving anything from God. This is a radical truth. God does not deprive anyone. The son received compassion, love, hugs, and kisses from his father. The father even threw a big party for him.

Remember, Jesus was the one who told this story. The word "worship" means "kissing." When worshiping in church, people lift their hands to kiss their Father God. Like babies or toddlers, they'll raise their hands and cry, "Papa." The father will lift the baby from the crib and kiss him. When we cry "Abba," He lifts us and kisses us. It does not matter if we are young or old; God calls us His children.

> For you did not receive the spirit of bondage again
> to fear, but you received the Spirit of adoption
> by whom we cry out, "Abba, Father." The Spirit
> Himself bears witness with our spirit that we are
> children of God, and if children, then heirs—heirs
> of God and joint heirs with Christ, if indeed we
> suffer with *Him*, that we may also be glorified to-
> gether.
>
> — Romans 8:15–17

EPILOGUE

The Catholic sat mesmerized while the other two pretended to mind their business. They listened, but they did not act interested. The Catholic's countenance was a look of awe and disbelief.

I told him that I never stopped believing in God and that He always cared for me despite the odds and opposition I faced. Everyone was quiet when I finished my story.

Hastily, the Catholic scooted his chair out. He got up and left rudely without saying a word. His colleagues followed suit. I slowly ate my cold dinner, feeling perplexed and wishing I never shared my story.

———————

My Salvation Army leader dropped me off at my post near the mall to work the following day. It was just after 9:30 a.m. It was a quiet and beautiful sunny morning. I closed my eyes and enjoyed the sun's warmth on my face. I breathed in slowly, the fresh, warm morning air into my lungs.

In the distance, I saw a young mother pushing a baby stroller. She was coming toward me with an inquisitive look on her face and stopped to ask me if my name was Morgan.

I did not recognize her. I thought to myself, *How does she know me?* I replied kindly with a smile, "Yes, I am Morgan. Have we met before?"

She replied, "No, but you talked with my father last night at the restaurant."

My eyes showed shock. "Is your father the Catholic?" I asked.

"Yes, that is him," she said, immediately bursting into tears. I stood there unsure of what was causing her to cry and wondered if this was a good or a bad thing.

The daughter pulled herself together and said, "I have been praying for my father's salvation for many years. He is not a serious Catholic. But he accepted Jesus into his heart right after hearing you share your story last night. It made him see God in a real way that he never believed God could do."

The tears in my eyes started to swell up as I stared at her with wonder. I did not know what to say. It all made sense to me why the Catholic dismissed himself abruptly from dinner the other night.

The daughter continued, "Your testimony changed his life." She quickly hugged me, looked at me sincerely, and said, "Thank you for sharing your story. This has been the best Christmas present I could ever ask for."

After she strolled away with her baby, there was a quiet lull for a few minutes…

I stood there in awe of what had transpired and how my story affected the Catholic man's life in a real way. It became clear to me then that not only did Jesus come looking for him to save his life, but mine, too. My mind wandered back to when I was a little girl as I recollected all those times when my screams were never heard. I realized then at that moment that Jesus did hear me. My eyes welled up with tears, and my heart was flooded with gratitude realizing that Jesus was with me all along and rescued me from the pit of hell. I looked up at the sky and said, "Thank You, Jesus," and then slowly, I glanced down at the Salvation Army display sign and read the words in a whisper, "for 'Doing the Most Good.'"

AFTERWORD:

Grace, Grace to It

I had numerous strongholds built up around my mind that left me dehumanized. The main ones were strongholds of rejection, hopelessness, and despair. They left me feeling lost as I sifted through all the ashes of the past, not knowing how to piece them together. In the middle of those bondages, I knew what I had to do. The first step was that I chose to forgive my father in person. It took a lot of guts for me to face him. I had a lot of heartache, but I decided to do it. Forgiveness was the first key in unlocking the prison door in my life.

After I had forgiven him, it was amazing how it transformed my father. Just showing him the love and grace of the Father above instantly drew him to accept Jesus into his heart. After my father's death, I was still going through the motions.

My mind was not completely transformed. It took many years for the Holy Spirit to chip away at the cemented strongholds that held me completely captive. I desperately wanted a better life and truly desired God to renew me, yet I was stuck. Self-sabotaging by overeating, self-pity, and depression made matters worse. The worst part was that those stuffy, suffocating, and oppressive churches I attended did nothing about it. I was told never to share my past, sweep it under the rug, and put on a pretend happy face. There was nobody that I could share or confide in. I had once asked for prayer for healing. The pastors put anointing oil on my head, prayed for one minute, and then it was business as usual for them. I never felt like my soul even mattered to them. My spiritual bank account was depleted.

I started listening to podcasts of two specific pastors that transformed my life even though I was told not to listen to them. I had never heard of anything like it before. The simple and true gospel of the grace of Jesus transformed my life. Strongholds melted away like wax. It took many years to break away from the legalism I had been asphyxiated by for so long. Still, by the grace of God, the Bible came alive and slowly transformed my mind and set loose false, heretical doctrines and wrong opinions not based on the Bible that had held me captive.

It came to a point when I had to speak to the mountains in my life as Zerubbabel did in Zechariah 4:7, "'Who *are* you, O great mountain? Before Zerubbabel *you shall become* a plain! And he shall bring forth the capstone with shouts of "Grace, grace to it!"'"

Before I moved to Houston, I literally "shook the dust off my feet" from the legalistic abuse I had endured for over twenty-seven years. I left the past behind feeling a complete sense of spiritual freedom.

I started growing at my new church and saw changes in my life. It is incredible how one pastor can ultimately determine people's destinies for the good or the bad. From my experience, there are bad pastors and good pastors.

Walking Out from the Prison Cell

Peter was therefore kept in prison, but constant prayer was offered to God for him by the church. And when Herod was about to bring him out, that night Peter was sleeping, bound with two chains between two soldiers; and the guards before the door were keeping the prison. Now behold, an angel of the Lord stood by him, and a light shone in the prison; and he struck Peter on the side and raised him up, saying, "Arise quickly!" And his chains fell off his hands. Then the angel said to him, "Gird yourself and tie on your sandals"; and so he did. And he said to him, "Put on your garment and follow me." So he went out and followed him, and did not know that what was done by the angel was real, but thought he was seeing a vision. When they were past the first and the second guard posts, they came to the iron gate that leads to the city, which opened to them of its own accord; and they went out and went down one street, and immediately the angel departed from him. And when Peter had come to himself, he said, "Now I know for certain that the Lord has sent His angel and has delivered me from the hand of Herod and from all the expectation of the Jewish people."

— Acts 12:5–11

To sum up, Peter is in prison for his faith, and his life is in Herod's hands, yet believers are praying for him. God hears their intercession for him, and an astonishing thing happens. An angel appears to him and tells Peter to rise and walk out of the prison cell. As Peter walks with the angel, every obstacle is removed, every yoke is broken, and every impenetrable door opens.

Peter walks out of his prison cell through the impossible passageways and past the guards and is set free. The scripture says that Peter did not believe what he was seeing. He thought he was dreaming, and all the while, he believed in his mind that he was in prison even though he was free.

What Peter experienced is like what many believers do. In John 8:36, it says, "Therefore if the Son makes you free, you shall be free indeed."

I have encountered many believers who doubt that. We can quote the Scriptures and inflate ourselves to look super spiritual, but most of us do not believe in God's promises in the Bible.

When I was unjustly put in jail in 2015, the physical surroundings did not make me feel free; therefore, I behaved as if I was in prison in my mind, too.

During my probation, I found a Christian counselor named Michelle who helped me see the power of Jesus to shake off my chains. If you do not believe you are free, you will never be free, even if you already are.

If I had not believed in the power of Jesus, I would still be living in chains today.

Once, my dog had a battery-operated collar synced to a wire underground that stretched along the fence line. It created an invisible boundary on the property. Each time my dog went on the boundary line, the collar would shock her. She quickly learned to stay in her confines because she did not want to get shocked. On one occasion, I took her collar off and set her free to run and play fetch with me outside the boundary lines. When I commanded her to come, she stopped precisely where the invisible fence line was. Even though I told her to come, she never dared to cross over because she believed she was not free. No matter how many times I told her she could come, she was determined to believe she was not free.

If you do not believe you are set free from a particular addiction, you will not be, and you will still struggle with it even though Jesus says you are free.

The Word of God is like a two-edged sword. When you read the Scriptures out loud, something happens in the spirit realm. Chains start to break. It is time to start treating the promises of God as the Word of God.

Time is of the essence to put a stop to living in jail, which we are already freed from. Jesus has unshackled and severed the heavy-laden iron-clad chains. The obstacles that have caused you to stay stuck have already been cleared.

Peter thought it was a dream, but it was no dream. It's time to wake up and believe the promises of God; see the chains fall off from your life. See yourself walking and passing the enemy's guard posts and walk away free because you are free indeed.

Restoration

When I discovered the book of Joel Chapter Two at Asbury College, it became my favorite book in the Bible and has been my anchor of hope. I had often meditated verses 25–27 so many times until it sank into my spirit.

> So I will restore to you the years that the swarm-
> ing locust has eaten,
> The crawling locust,
> The consuming locust,
> And the chewing locust,
> My great army which I sent among you.
> You shall eat in plenty and be satisfied,
> And praise the name of the LORD your God,
> Who has dealt wondrously with you;
> And My people shall never be put to shame.
> Then you shall know that I am in the midst of
> Israel:
> I am the LORD your God
> And there is no other.
> My people shall never be put to shame.
>
> — Joel 2:25–27

A few years later, upon graduation from seminary in Guatemala, Central America, a prophecy was prayed over me in Spanish:

> Restoration, restoration, My daughter, is the work
> I have been doing in your life. The order has been
> given to restore this temple, to restore this abode,
> My daughter. Do not fear restoration. Everything
> will be made new, My daughter, and even much
> better than before. Restoration is the work I have

been doing in your life. The result will be finished because the King has decided, My daughter. The King has been so determined. Your eyes will see the total restoration, My daughter, says your God.

Upon hearing those words, my heart was flooded with tears of joy. It was surreal that God knew the longing in my heart for restoration that these exact words were prayed over me. Since then, I have been looking forward to God fulfilling His promise to restore everything stolen and destroyed in my life. Miracles have come to pass, and there are more things that I am looking forward to with expectancy. God is in the restoration business.

There was one specific request that I had prayed for many times as a young adult. I prayed earnestly to God to restore my virginity stolen from my father. God did a physical miracle during my quondam marriage and restored my virginity.

Isaiah 53:5 says, "But He was wounded for our transgressions, He was bruised for our iniquities; The chastisement for our peace was upon Him, and by His stripes, we are healed."

In other words, the stripes on Jesus's back were lashed and whipped unmercifully so that we all could be healed. The verse does not say that we *will* be healed, nor does it give us any conditions on what we must do to receive healing. Simply, it clearly states that we *are* healed. All we must do is agree and believe in God's Word that we are already healed even though we have not received it yet. Romans 4:17 says, "God, who gives life to the dead and calls those things which do not exist as though they did."

Speak the promises from the Scriptures as though they have already happened to you because God promises in Jeremiah 1:12 that He is actively watching over His Word to fulfill it.

Jesus Is Crossing the Sea Right Now to Save You

Align yourself with the Word of God and believe what He says is true. Jesus can restore all your life's emotional, mental, physical, and spiritual damages.

There was a demon-possessed man mentioned in the book of Luke 8:22–39. This is one of my favorite stories. If you like to watch scary horror thriller movies, this scenario in the Bible will beat them all! I'm not a fan of scary movies, yet this is based on a true story about a naked demon-possessed man from the tombs. He hung out at a graveyard in the Gadarenes, near the Sea of Galilee. The man would run around the tombs day and night without any clothes.

Imagine if you went to pay your respects to a loved one who died and was buried at the Gadarenes Graveyard. Out of nowhere, a strange figure appears behind a tomb and runs toward you, screaming. I'm pretty sure that would be the last time you would go there.

As the story continues, Jesus wanted to sail to the region of the Gadarenes. So, He and the disciples set out, and as they sailed, Jesus fell asleep.

A dangerous windstorm came down on the sea, filling it with so much water. The disciples woke Jesus, saying, "Master, Master, we are perishing!" And He awoke and rebuked the wind and the raging waves, and they ceased, and there was a calm.

Jesus said, "Where's your faith?" The disciples were so afraid and astonished that He commanded the winds and water to obey Him.

The disciples did not know that the enemy did not want Jesus and them to go to the other side of the sea where demons had possessed a man. This was the enemy's territory. Jesus knew He was not wanted there. The enemy sent the storm, but Jesus rebuked it.

The demon-possessed man had been seized many times by the unclean spirit. The man was kept under guard and bound with chains and shackles, but he would break the bonds and be driven by the demon into the desert.

As the boat was getting nearer to the land, I'm sure the disciples were shocked at what they witnessed. When Jesus stepped onto the shore, a naked man ran to Him screaming. I imagine he was wild out of his mind. When he saw Jesus, he cried out and fell before Him and said with a loud voice, "What have You to do with me, Jesus, Son of the Most High God? I beg You, do not torment me."

Jesus had commanded the unclean spirit to come out of the man. Jesus then asked him, "What is your name?" And he said "Legion," for many demons had entered him. And they begged Jesus not to command them to depart into the abyss. Instead, they begged Him to let them enter a large herd of pigs that were feeding there on the hillside. So, Jesus permitted them.

The demons came out of the man and entered the pigs, and the herd rushed down the steep bank into the sea and drowned.

Imagine the scenario of the swine squealing, snorting, and scrambling down into the water and drowning to death. When the legion of demons entered their bodies unannounced, it had to have been so forceful that it would have induced them to end their lives.

But, when the herders saw what had happened, they fled and told it in the city and in the country. Then people went out to see what had happened, and they came to Jesus and found the man from whom the demons had gone, sitting at the feet of Jesus, clothed and in his right mind, and they were afraid.

The man was sitting at the feet of Jesus. He was deeply thankful for what Jesus had done for him. He did not want to let go of Him.

All the people asked Jesus to leave because they were seized with great fear. So, He got into the boat and returned. The delivered man begged Jesus to be with him, but Jesus sent him away, saying, "Return to your home, and declare how much God has done for you." The man went away, proclaiming throughout the whole city how much Jesus had done for him.

If you are seized with shame, panic attacks, fear, hopelessness, or despair, or if you are bound by addictions or tormented by other forms of abuse, there is One who will come unafraid to save you. Jesus is not afraid of the storm because His name is the Prince of Peace. He is not afraid of the dark because He is the Light of the World. He is not afraid to go down into the deepest and darkest pits of hell to set the captives free because He is the Resurrection and the Life.

Jesus will stop any storm in His way to find and rescue you. Jesus will break every chain and send the demons to flight. Jesus has paid the price for your healing. No matter what demon you face, Jesus is now crossing the sea to save you.